CREATIVE WAYS TO OFFER PRAISE

100 Ideas for Sunday Worship

Lisa Flinn and Barbara Younger

Abingdon Press

Nashville

CREATIVE WAYS TO OFFER PRAISE
100 Ideas for Sunday Worship

Copyright © 1993 by Abingdon Press

This book is printed on recycled, acid-free paper.

Library of Congress Cataloging-in-Publication Data

Flinn, Lisa, 1951-
  Creative ways to offer praise : 100 ideas for Sunday worship / Lisa Flinn and Barbara Younger.
    p.   cm
  ISBN 0-687-09845-9 (acid-free paper)
  1. Public worship.   I. Younger, Barbara, 1954-   II. Title.
  BV15.F577   1993
  264—dc20   92-36733
                                                                    CIP

Scripture quotations, unless otherwise noted, are from the New Revised Standard Version of the Bible, copyright 1989 by the Division of Christian Education of the National Council of the Churches of Christ in the USA. Used by permission.

Those noted KJV are from the King James Version of the Bible.

Layout and Design: John Boegel

96 97 98 99 00 01 02 03 04 — 10 9 8 7 6 5 4 3

MANUFACTURED IN THE UNITED STATES OF AMERICA

**To our parents—
Shirley and Maurice Harrison
and
Nancy and Ernest Kiehne**

CONTENTS

INTRODUCTION

As children made in the image of a creating God, we are creative people. Let's celebrate this gift by offering our praise in creative ways!

An interdenominational book, *CREATIVE WAYS TO OFFER PRAISE: 100 Ideas for Sunday Worship* is brimming with simple yet meaningful ideas designed to enhance a Christian worship service without changing the actual order of worship.

This book provides options for church decorations, processionals and recessionals, bring-in gifts and offerings, greetings, readings and responses, children's activities, prayers, sermons, Holy Communion and fellowship foods, and worship mementos. The ideas are inspired by passages of Scripture, the church calendar, Christian history, age-old traditions, and the customs and challenges of today's world.

Directed to pastors and others who plan the worship service, this flexible resource invites Sunday school classes, youth groups, men's and women's organizations, and church committees to take an active part in Sunday worship.

Intended to touch Christians of any age, *CREATIVE WAYS TO OFFER PRAISE* will bring worshipers closer to God and to one another. Children are carefully drawn into the worship service and made to feel a welcome part of it. Even adults, who sometimes resist change, won't be able to resist a Favorite Hymn Contest, Emergency Verses, or a Jumble Prayer!

With great respect for the traditions of Christian worship throughout the centuries, we offer these ideas, some old and some new, for the Sundays in your church's future.

Lisa Flinn
Barbara Younger
Hillsborough, North Carolina

1. VISUAL TOUCHES

STILL LIFE

A still life display sets a mood from the moment it is beheld and visually draws the beholder into the spirit of the worship service. The occasion might be your church's anniversary, the first day of spring, a visit from a missionary, or the end of vacation church school. Still lifes can be created from a combination of all sorts of objects. Here are some suggestions:

Seasonal Harvests:
Fall: leaves, gourds, Indian corn, pumpkins
Winter: evergreen, winter berries, bare branches, pinecones
Spring: sprigs of flowering bushes or trees, empty bird's nests, decorated eggs
Summer: flowers, fruit, seashells, grasses

Historical Artifacts:
To celebrate an anniversary of your church, denomination, or town, consider antiques, collectibles, periodicals, photographs, and documents from the era in which it was founded.

Dolls and Toys:
For World Communion Sunday or a mission project, display international dolls; to celebrate Noah's Ark, a grouping of toy animals; to raise money for Habitat for Humanity, small toy houses or dollhouses.

Books:
Old or unusual Bibles, hymnals, books of Bible stories, illustrated books on a specific subject, or books from your church library can be displayed. Some books can be opened to an interesting page, others closed to show their covers.

Musical Instruments:
These are especially appropriate when music is a special part of the service, such as a flute solo or a visiting bagpiper.

Mission Work:
Collect objects from the region of the world where your church's

missionary or a guest speaker is working. A variety of international objects is also effective.

Church Memorabilia:

Any artifacts relating to the church such as old directories, photographs, record books, or scrapbooks will make a fitting exhibit.

Art:

Crafts and artwork made in Sunday school, vacation church school, or prepared for an upcoming bazaar make a creative still life. Encourage artists in your congregation by displaying their work.

Once you determine what sorts of objects are needed for the still life you want to create, you can plan how to gather them. Place a note in the bulletin or newsletter stating what types of items you need. Many people enjoy sharing their collections. Ask to be contacted by a certain date in order to know in plenty of time what items are available and when they should be brought to the church. All items should be labeled discreetly, perhaps with initials marked on small pieces of masking tape. Take special care to guard valuables against loss or damage.

Still lifes can be set up on an altar or communion table, if this is permissible in your church, on tables in the front or back of the church, in windows, or in entrance ways. You may want to cover the table with a tablecloth, quilt, or fabric that suits the theme.

The still life should be arranged well before the service begins. Rearranging the objects may be necessary until you achieve a display that suits your eye. Step back and look at the arrangement to make sure that it is effective from a distance.

Place a note in the bulletin explaining the purpose of the still life and telling a little bit about the objects displayed. After the service worshipers should be encouraged to examine the still life more closely and to ask any questions they might have about the objects. In some cases you may want to leave a still life in place for several Sundays.

BULLETIN COVERS

Hand-decorated covers for worship bulletins help set the tone for a worship service the moment they are received from an usher or greeter. Sunday school classes and youth groups will enjoy making covers, and adults in women's or men's groups could also have fun with this project. Within your congregation you may even have an individual who would like to design and create bulletin covers for a Sunday service.

Determine how many bulletins your church uses per Sunday. In a large church you may want to make covers for just one service. Construction paper, colored bond, or plain white paper can be folded in half and the regular bulletin placed or stapled inside. If your church uses a larger bulletin, two sheets of paper can be stapled together.

Designs may cover the entire piece of paper or just the front half. They should be simple enough so that it won't be difficult to make lots of covers.

Handmade bulletin covers are appropriate for special occasions, but will also add an enriching touch to any Sunday service. Here are some suggestions for mediums that work well:

Blot Paintings:
Drop splotches of paint on one half of the paper, fold, and rub to create interesting designs. Marker or crayon can be used to trace around the blots and turn them into butterflies, flowers, fish, or crosses.

Paint Prints:
Sponges can be cut into the shapes of fish, hearts, stars, crosses, and other Christian symbols, dipped into paint, and used to make prints. Natural objects such as shells, leaves, flowers, and vegetables also create effective prints.

Cutouts:
Fabric scraps, wallpaper, wrapping paper, and newspaper can be cut into a variety of shapes from anchors to doves and glued to paper. Even young children can cut pictures from magazines or greeting cards that show the wonders of God's creation or gifts for which they are thankful.

Rubbings:
Use crayons to make rubbings of keys, shells, coins, and other Christian symbols. Words and symbols engraved on old tombstones can also be used for a rubbing.

Watercolors:
Simple paintings of the sea, flowers, rainbows, or mountains are lovely when done with watercolors.

Be certain that any paint or glue is completely dry before you stack the bulletin covers together. Place a note in the bulletin itself explaining the significance of the cover and thanking the artists.

CANDLES

The lighting of candles is a beautiful element of worship, whether done weekly or just on special occasions. A unique and interesting way to bring candlelight into your worship service is to ask members of different groups within the congregation to bring in a candlestick, with a candle, on a designated Sunday. The eclectic mixture of silver, wood, brass, ceramics, and glass, as well as the varying colors and heights of the candles, will create a medley of light for all to behold. Plan how the candles will be presented and lit. They may be put in place before the service and lit by an acolyte, or the group may process in carrying the candles. You may want to incorporate some of these Scripture readings about light into the service: Matthew 5:14-16, John 8:12, Romans 13:11-12, Ephesians 5:8.

Another way to use candles in worship is to celebrate Candlemas. This old festival was observed about forty days after Christmas. The Gospel of Luke describes the baby Jesus' first visit to the Temple, as was customary under Jewish law. The old man Simeon was promised by the Holy Spirit that he would see the Messiah before his death. On the very day that Mary and Joseph brought their baby son to the Temple, Simeon was guided by the Holy Spirit to go there. Simeon held Jesus in his arms and called him "a light for revelation to the Gentiles" (see Luke 2:22-34).

To celebrate Candlemas at your church, give candles to the worshipers as they come into the church. Candles may be lit by ushers or acolytes during a prayer or the closing hymn. Encourage the congregation to take these candles home to burn during meals or prayers.

PAPER BANNERS

Although cloth banners are lovely and will stay in good condition for a long time, paper banners are inexpensive, can be simple and fun to make, and can even be made of recycled materials. Consider the back of used computer paper, paper bags, or even newspapers. Pictures from magazines, wallpaper, construction paper, crayons, or paint can be used to illustrate a beloved Bible verse or story, celebrate a season of the church year, or mark the close of vacation church school. Paper banners can be hung just about anywhere from the balcony to the door of the church. Here are just a few ideas:

Cut and flatten brown grocery bags and have the toddlers glue on a simple shape, such as a triangle to represent the Trinity for Trinity Sunday, the first Sunday after Pentecost.

Sheets of newspaper can be decorated with poster paints. Use bold letters to write words such as "Peace: John 14:27" or "Good News: Mark 16:20."

Trace around each child in Sunday school, have them cut out their outlines, and add faces and paper wings. The Sunday school children become angels! Hang the outlines from rafters, walls, or even trees outside the church door.

Remember that part of the charm of paper banners is that they need not, and probably should not, be hung for too long. Take them down after one or several Sundays and toss them away. That's the joy of a banner made for pennies from paper.

FLOWERS AND OTHER ARRANGEMENTS FROM NATURE

In Psalm 65:11 David writes "You crown the year with your bounty." Throughout the year, wherever you live, you will find a great variety of flowers, herbs, vines, shrubs, and other plants that can be made into arrangements. Even if your church usually uses florist arrangements, consider asking members of your congregation to create their own arrangements as an inexpensive alternative to purchased flowers. Almost anything that grows from God's earth can be used in some way as an interesting, thought-provoking, and eye-catching arrangement.

Along with bowls and vases, jars, pitchers, crocks, tins, and baskets can be used to hold arrangements. Some arrangements need not be placed in a container but can be laid directly on the altar or communion table, in windows, or wherever you choose. Below are some suggestions:

Arrange a variety of wildflowers or other plants that grow within a few miles of the church.

Use grapevines or other vines to represent Jesus' words, "I am the vine, you are the branches" (John 15:5).

Arrange single blossoms in small bottles or jars.

During the week of St. John's Eve (June 23), hang branches of herbs about your church as were hung in homes and barns in the Middle Ages in honor of John the Baptist.

For a healing service or a Sunday when a story of the healing miracles is read, bring in herbs used to aid healing in centuries past: lemon balm, mint, parsley, foxglove, or feverfew.

In the spring, bring in pots of seeds just beginning to sprout. The seedlings can then be sent to members of the church who are sick or infirm.

For Holy Week, cactus, thistle, or other thorny branches represent the crown of thorns placed on the head of Jesus.

In the fall, bring gourds into the church. In days gone by, gourds were associated both with Jonah and with the Resurrection.

For a change from plants, display goldfish swimming in crystal clear bowls to celebrate the creatures of God's bountiful earth!

HYMNAL MARKERS

Most people, from beginning readers to folks with bifocals, like to mark the pages in their hymnals to avoid fumbling when the music begins. Simple hymnal markers are not only appreciated by the congregation, but add a subtle touch of color to the church. Have the markers placed in the hymnals before the worshipers arrive and allow a bit of the marker, and any ribbon used, to show from the top of the hymnal. Here are some easy and affordable suggestions:

Wallpaper:
Sample wallpaper books and closeout sales provide a free or inexpensive selection of paper for hymnal markers. You may opt to use a variety of florals or only a particular color, or you may find paper with printed hearts or another symbol. A roll of wide border paper will have a more finished look and will be the easiest to cut. A paper cutter will do the job quickly, but pinking shears will give a festive touch.

Ribbon:
A simple slip of satin, grosgrain, or cotton craft ribbon in the liturgical color of the season is quick but elegant. The use of ribbon may be more costly, but these hymnal markers will last for years and can even be washed and pressed. Cut the lengths three to four inches longer than the hymnal so that the ribbon shows at top and bottom.

Watercolor Paper:
The heavy weight of this paper makes it quite durable. Because of the weight and texture of the paper, it is attractive left undecorated. If you choose to decorate it, a free form design such as a wash, blot, or spattering of paint will make decorating fast and fun.

Clear Contact Paper:
Usually available in housewares departments, this paper is perfect for creating see-through hymnal markers. Consider mustard seeds, leaves, dried flowers, blades of grass, or confetti.

If your congregation enjoys using the hymnal markers, when they wear out or for a change, make another set.

AISLE DECORATIONS

Have you ever watched as a flower girl sprinkled flowers or flower petals on the floor as she walked down the aisle? The flowers were a delight to the eye, and the idea of a bride treading on a flower-strewn path was charming. Why not borrow this wedding custom and bring it into the worship of God? Aisle decorations offer a simple way to create a mood, express a theme, and even involve the congregation.

Each of the ideas listed below is based on a passage of Scripture, which may be used as a greeting from greeters or ushers or in a call to worship or opening prayer. The verse may also be printed in the bulletin.

Crosses:
"But if we walk in the light as he himself is in the light, we have fellowship with one another, and the blood of Jesus his Son cleanses us from all sin" (1 John 1:7). Use colored tape to make crosses down the aisle. A youth group or Sunday school class would love to help with this. A Communion Sunday is a good time to use this design.

Confetti:
"There is one body and one Spirit . . . one Lord, one faith, one baptism, one God and Father of all, who is above all and through all and in all" (Ephesians 4:4-6). Use squares of netting or tissue paper and a length of yarn or ribbon to tie up small bundles of paper confetti. The bundles may be given to a particular group to open and sprinkle in the aisles or to all worshipers as they walk to their seats. Try confetti for a baptism, New Member's Sunday, a Commissioning Sunday, or Youth Sunday.

Hearts:
"Teach me your way, O LORD, that I may walk in your truth; give me an undivided heart to revere your name" (Psalm 86:11). Cut out construction paper hearts about one inch in size. Hearts any larger may cause someone to slip. Hearts are just right for the presentation of Bibles, Teacher Appreciation Sunday, or even ordinations.

Adding Machine Tape:
"The fruit of the Spirit is love, joy, peace, patience, kindness, generosity, faithfulness, gentleness, and self-control" (Galatians 5:22).

This paper gives a dramatic effect when rolled down the length of the aisle. Secure the paper at both ends of the aisle with a piece of masking tape. The list of words found in this verse should be repeated in colorful bold print down the entire length of paper. This is a great project for a youth group or Sunday school class and is appropriate anytime.

Flowers and Leaves:
The plants are listed along with their meaning and a Scripture verse that may be associated with them.
Lilies of the valley: Advent of Christ (John 4:25)
Pansies: Remembrance (1 Corinthians 11:24)
Violets: Humility (Philippians 2:3)
White columbines: The Holy Spirit (Matthew 10:16)
Dandelions: One of the bitter herbs (Exodus 12:8)
Cherry: The sweetness of God (1 Timothy 6:18)
Clover: The Trinity (Matthew 28:19)
Palms: Victory (John 12:12-13)
Cedar: Christ and his kingdom (Ezekiel 17:22)
In a processional, individuals may sprinkle flowers or leaves from small baskets. Larger baskets work well when the flowers or leaves are being given to the whole congregation. Arrange for ushers to offer the flowers or leaves to worshipers as they enter the church. The worshipers may then be asked to drop the flowers or leaves as they walk down the aisle or to save them and fling them into the aisles when instructed to do so after the verse is read during the service.

PARAMENTS

Almost all churches have paraments that enhance their pulpit, lectern, and altar or communion tables. These paraments, usually coordinated with the liturgical color of the season, are often decorated with embroidery or appliqué. For an eye-catching change of pace, create your own paraments. Here are some ideas:

Fabric, table linens, or scarves from Europe, South America, Africa, or the Orient, add an international flair for World Communion Sunday, a visiting missionary, or a peacemaking service. Consider, too, Native American rugs, weavings, and embroidery.
Old sheets and fabric remnants can be cut to the right size and tie-dyed, batik-dyed, or painted. Designs can also be cut from paper or cloth and glued to the fabric.

Newspapers printed in other languages such as Korean or Japanese are easily obtained in some areas of the country. They make interesting paraments for a Sunday when verses about the Tower of Babel, Pentecost, or the Great Commission appear in the lectionary.

Quilts and other old cloths add an authentic touch to an anniversary celebration. Empty feed and seed bags are perfect for Rogation Days, the three days before Ascension Day that celebrate the planting of the spring crops.

Netting, available at fabric stores, can be filled with paper fish and hung from the lectern and pulpit to remind us that Jesus calls us to "fish for people" (Matthew 4:19).

PATCHWORK FOR THE PASTOR

Your pastor touches the life of each church member through prayer, preaching, teaching, visitation, and through all the other work that he or she does in the church. Why not symbolize this connection with a patchwork stole made of squares of fabric donated by members of the congregation? This very personalized gift can be given in honor of the pastor's birthday, to celebrate his or her call to your congregation, or to mark the pastor's years in the ministry, whether it's five or fifty.

This patchwork stole may be worn at various times over the course of the year and the pastor will also be pleased to wear it when he or she is a guest speaker at another church. Of course, the stole will also be a fine keepsake of his or her years at your church.

Making the stole will go well if the project is put in the hands of seamstresses or quilters who will feel comfortable with the task.

The traditional stole is about 5 inches by 96 inches, or 480 square inches. Allowing for a half-inch seam allowance on all four sides of the fabric, each finished square will be one-inch square. Therefore, the squares brought in by the congregation should be two-inch squares.

In smaller churches, you may need each family to contribute several squares. In larger churches, each family may need to contribute only one square. You may even gather enough squares so that the stole's backing can be made of patchwork too.

After the squares are gathered, sew small rows of five squares with a half-inch seam allowance. Make as many five-square rows as possible, then begin to create the length of the stole by sewing the small rows together along their width. If you have fewer than 480 squares, divide the amount evenly to form each end of the stole and use a single strip of plain muslin or a calico print around the neck to create the necessary length.

Back the stole with plain muslin or a calico print and finish by quilting, top stitching, or tacking.

Last, but not least, write the date the stole is presented and who the gift is from on the back of the stole with a fabric pen or embroidery floss.

TABLEAUX

A tableau is a scene staged by participants in costume. Since there are no lines to be learned or music to be sung, tableaux can be put together without rehearsal. Effective costumes are the key, although they need not be elaborate and props can be kept to a minimum. Stage a tableau before or after a worship service, either outdoors, in a large hallway or entrance, or in the church. A note in the bulletin can explain the significance of the tableau, if necessary, and perhaps list the names of the participants. Here are a few ideas:

The Christmas Story:
Many churches already have costumes for the Christmas story, usually in children's sizes. If you have lots of kids, they can take turns being part of the tableau on the various Sundays of Advent. If you have few children, or just one class is to participate, consider having the angels one week, the shepherds the next, then Mary and Joseph, and finally, the Magi.

International Costumes:
These are especially appropriate for World Communion Sunday or a visit from a missionary. Perhaps the participants can link arms as a gesture of Christian unity throughout the world.

Lent:
During Lent, stage some of the events of Holy Week such as the Last Supper, Jesus and his disciples at the Garden of Gethsemane, or the women and angel at the empty tomb.

Finally, if your church is putting on a more elaborate drama or musical, consider using some of the costumed players in a tableau as publicity for the actual performance.

2. PROCESSIONALS AND RECESSIONALS

BRANCHES, BOUGHS, AND GRASSES

A processional into God's house with palms, branches, or other bits of nature will call worshipers to focus on a symbolic representation of their faith. The choir, the children, or the entire congregation may process into church bringing the beauty of creation in their hands. These branches, boughs, or grasses may be held during the worship service or spread on the altar or communion table.

While palms are most closely associated with processionals, other greens have a traditional symbolic meaning in worship:

Palm: victory (Palm Sunday)
Cedar: Christ and his kingdom (Christ the King Sunday)
Holly: Christ's crown of thorns (Holy Week)
Oak: strength of faith (Pentecost)
Willow: the gospel of Christ (Week of Christian Unity)
Orange: purity, charity, and generosity (stewardship)
Olive: peace (World Communion Sunday)
Laurel: triumph, eternity, and chastity (Palm Sunday and Easter)
Myrtle: immortality and divine generosity (Ascension)
Fern: humility and sincerity (any communion Sunday)
Wheat: bounty of the earth; in communion, the bread of life (Thanksgiving, Rogation, any communion Sunday)
Bulrush: the multitudes who live humbly by the "living waters of Jesus" (New Member Sunday, Homecoming)

Although suggested times when you might want to use specific greens are listed, they may be used on any Sunday you choose. Be sure to put a note in the bulletin giving the significance of the green.

Remember that although processionals are most often done with the singing of a hymn, a silent procession has great dignity too.

PROCESSIONAL PENNANTS

Pennants are great fun to wave at a football game, but a Christian pennant can also be waved in a processional. Locate inexpensive dowels, bamboo garden stakes, or sticks from the yard, and tie, stitch, or glue fabric to them. For a simpler pennant, use paper and a straw. Decorate pennants with crayon, marker, paint, or cutouts.

Children love to wave pennants in a procession, but take care that they are carefully spaced to avoid accidental pokes and jabs. For adults, small pennants may be rested in the hymnal and carried in this fashion in a procession as the opening hymn is sung. Liturgical colors, Christian symbols, or words such as "Alleluia" work well on pennants. Here is one suggestion:

Clouds are appropriate for Ascension since Jesus ascended into heaven on a cloud, and also for Transfiguration Sunday, the last Sunday after Epiphany, since God's voice came from a cloud. Glue white clouds onto blue fabric or paper.

THE CROSS

Since Jesus first carried his own cross to Calvary, processional crosses have been carried in remembrance of the death and resurrection of Jesus. Processional crosses are available through Christian catalogs, and many churches use a cross in their processional and recessional each Sunday. If this is not the custom at your church, consider using a processional cross, perhaps on a special occasion such as Easter, or near Holy Cross Day, which in earlier centuries was celebrated on September 14 as a time outside of the Easter season to honor the symbol of the cross.

Ask a young person to carry the cross in a solemn fashion to the front of the church, where it can be rested against the lectern or pulpit or another suitable location.

There are many ways to fashion a processional cross. Here are two:

With twine, lash a shorter piece of wood to a longer one. Use sticks found in the woods or wood from a lumber yard.

Ask a frame shop if they will give you two strips of matting board. The strips can be glued together to form a cross. Paint the cross or twist strips of fabric or ribbon around it. Secure the cross to a thin curtain rod or dowel using strong tape.

ANGELS, SHEPHERDS, AND OTHER COSTUMES

Where are all those costumes from the plays of past years? Retrieve them from the storage boxes or closet and give them a new use—the processional. Children will be delighted with the opportunity to wear costumes without needing to learn a script. Adults who have a dramatic flair may also enjoy participating in a costumed processional.

If your costumes are suited to a specific Bible story, such as Noah's Ark (animals) or the Creation (stars, sun, birds, fish), then consult the lectionary to determine a time when a processional with these costumes can be linked with the scripture readings.

Of course, angels and shepherds are perfect for the Advent season, but you may want to use angels to celebrate Michaelmas, which commemorates all angels (around September 29), and shepherds for Good Shepherd Sunday, the fourth Sunday of Easter.

Costumed processionals are great for including a number of people, but don't overlook the ease of using one, two, or three people in costume. Plan to have the Magi on Epiphany Sunday and other Bible characters and religious figures throughout the year.

AN OUTDOOR DISMISSAL

Closing a worship service by going outside into God's world can remind worshipers of their connection to creation. Singing the last verse of "This Is My Father's World" or hearing the words of a psalm while standing under the sky is both appropriate and reverent.

For a closing prayer outdoors, Psalm 148 works perfectly as it calls on all creatures and elements of creation to praise God. For an outdoor benediction, consider Psalm 121:8, Isaiah 40:3-8, or Genesis 9:12-16. Hymnbooks and Christian songbooks are filled with music that is enriched by an outdoor setting.

In years gone by, when farming and rural life created a common bond among parishioners, blessings of the animals and blessings of the crops were a part of church life. Rogation Day was a time to bless the spring planting. Rogation Day still holds meaning in today's world where the home garden often replaces the family farm and where the concern for the environment creates a common bond among all Christians. Celebrate Rogation Day, traditionally held forty days after Easter, by asking an outdoor blessing on the earth, the seeds and their harvest, and the efforts of the farmers and gardeners who work the soil of the earth.

DEPARTURE IN SILENCE

O
ften, it's the quiet moments in which God's presence touches us most deeply. On occasion, ask the congregation to depart in silence and not to speak until they have left the church. The pastor or lay leader may choose to say the following benediction before the congregation is dismissed:

> "This morning when you leave this place of worship, go in silence. As in the stillness of the night, the quiet of the dawn, listen for the voice of God as it touches your heart and makes you mindful of his love for you. May God bless you and keep you in the moments and the hours and the days ahead. In the name of the Father and of the Son and of the Holy Comforter. *Amen.*"

PASSING THE WORD

J
ust as the reading of the Good Book calls people together, it can also be called upon to dismiss them. After a benediction that speaks of God's Holy Word, such as Psalm 119:103-105 or 1 Peter 1:23-25, a Bible may be passed from worshiper to worshiper as a means of dismissing the congregation.

The pastor will hand a Bible to each section of pews, beginning at the front of the church, explaining that the word of God will be passed reverently from one person to another, along the pew, then on to the next pew, continuing until all have held the Bible and "passed the word." As a worshiper hands the Bible to the next person, he or she should say "[God's] word is a lamp to my feet" (Psalm 119:105) or "the word of the Lord endures forever" (1 Peter 1:25), and then get up and leave. The last persons will return the Bibles to the pastor as they leave the church.

LIGHTING THE WAY

I
n Ephesians 5:8 Paul calls Christians to "live as children of light." Reinforce this thought by using candles to escort worshipers out of the church at the close of the service. Depending on the size of your church, you will need from four to ten people to serve as ushers. Each of these ushers will need a ten- to twelve-inch candle. Fit each candle with a circle of heavy paper to serve as a drip protector.

Before the benediction, ask the ushers to come forward. Announce to the congregation that this Sunday they will be escorted from the service by candlelight. Each row should wait until the usher nods to follow him or her out of the church.

Following these instructions, the pastor or lay leader can use Paul's words from Ephesians as a benediction:

For once you were darkness, but now in the Lord you are light. Live as children of light—for the fruit of the light is found in all that is good and right and true.
Ephesians 5:8-9

If your church doesn't usually use candles, have them lit for this Sunday. The ushers should then come forward and light their candles from those in the front of the church. Starting with the first pew, the ushers will approach the row on either side of the church and say, "In the Lord you are light. Live as children of light." The usher will then nod for that row to follow him or her to the back of the church. When the church is empty, the ushers can extinguish all of the candles.

BIRTHDAY GOOD-BYE

The word "good-bye" is a contraction of "God be with ye." The true meaning of this expression is often lost today as people wave a hand and simply say, "Bye!" Involve the congregation in faithful farewells by asking them to say "God be with you" as the worshipers are dismissed by the months of their birth.

As each month is called out and the worshipers born in that month get up to leave, everyone else is to say "God be with you." Remind those born in December that although they are the last to leave the church, they are able to celebrate their birthday in the same month that Christians celebrate the birth of Jesus!

SHAKING HANDS

In most congregations the pastor shakes hands with the worshipers at the close of the service. Why not invite others to help with this pleasant task, perhaps one Sunday a month? Be certain to announce in the bulletin or from the pulpit which group is shaking hands. Those shaking hands should give their names to everyone they greet. Name tags are a good idea too. Think about recruiting:

> *Sunday school classes:* This is a great way to make sure that the young and the old are properly introduced at your church.

Church committees and organizations: This is a perfect opportunity for a group to recruit new members.

The choir: Oftentimes choir members rush to take off their robes and don't reappear until many worshipers are gone. Let the congregation have the chance to say a word of thanks to those whose music enhances worship week after week.

Individuals: New members, returning collegiates or service people, newlyweds, former members back to visit, the kids who just finished a week at church camp, or the family sitting in the third row can all be asked to greet the congregation with a handshake.

3. BRING-INS AND OFFERINGS

GROUP BOUQUET

Any season of the year, your congregation can create a group bouquet. On a specified Sunday, ask each worshiper to bring in a cutting from a flower, herb, shrub, decorative grass, or tree to contribute to the bouquet. Have someone stationed to greet the worshipers and to casually arrange the cuttings. Or, you may want to have each worshiper slip his or her cutting into the awaiting container. As you think about what you will use to hold the cuttings, be creative. Baskets, crockery, and large pitchers work well.

What a group bouquet might include:

Spring: flowering bulbs and shrubs, violets, dandelions, clover, buttercups, perennial herbs, ferns, and fruit tree prunings
Summer: flowering annuals and wildflowers, garden herbs, roses, flowering bulbs, and vines of flowers and fruit
Autumn: decorative grasses, chrysanthemums and other later blooming perennials and bulbs, wildflowers, honesty, strawflowers and other dried flowers, and sprigs of autumn leaves
Winter: cactus flowers, evergreen boughs, sprigs of boxwood, holly, or red twig dogwood, clusters of berries such as dogwood, juniper, bittersweet, or autumn olive

No matter what time of the year you call for a group bouquet or what part of the country you live in, you will find your church's group bouquet to be as colorful and interesting as the members of your church!

CAN COLLECTION SUNDAY

Collecting cans for a local food bank or shelter is an easy way for your congregation to help feed the hungry in your community. Designate a Sunday to be Can Collection Sunday. Print notices several weeks ahead of time in the bulletin and newsletter. Collages of magazine photographs of food or even actual labels soaked from cans will make eye-catching posters. Locate several large baskets or other attractive containers to be placed at the front of the church for the can collection.

Consider presenting a brief skit based on the familiar passage of Matthew 25:35-45 before the cans are collected. Recruit someone to play the part of Jesus and two or three people to be "the righteous."

THE SKIT

(Jesus is seated and the righteous are to the right of him.)

Jesus: In the kingdom of heaven, the Son of Man will say to those on his right hand, "I was hungry and you gave me food, I was thirsty and you gave me drink, I was a stranger and you welcomed me."

The Righteous *(in unison)*: Lord, when did we see you hungry and feed you or thirsty and give you drink, and when did we see you as a stranger and welcome you?

Jesus *(slowly)*: Truly I say to you, just as you did this to one of the least of my brethren, you did it also to me.

Encourage the players to memorize their lines, but if they are reluctant they can read them from slips of paper.

On Can Collection Sunday, as worshipers arrive with their cans, ask them to keep the cans with them in the pews.

When it is time for the skit, if you have decided to present one, introduce the players and explain that the skit is based on Matthew 25:35-45. After the skit, invite the congregation to come forward and place the cans in the baskets.

Sometime after the service, the cans can be delivered to the food bank or shelter.

GRAPEVINE COLLAGE

Jesus says "I am the vine, you are the branches" (John 15:5) when he speaks of his connection to his followers. Capture this thought by creating a grapevine collage of your congregation. Ask each family to bring in a photograph, either studio or snapshot, to donate to the collage. Set up a box or basket in the back of the church that can be used to collect the photographs.

When all the photographs have been gathered, turn them into grapes! Mount each one on a piece of purple colored paper six inches in circumference. If you can't locate purple paper, usually available at office supply stores, the Sunday school children can color white paper purple while they listen to a story or music.

Next, mount the grapes onto a large piece of poster board in the shape of a bunch of grapes. One piece of poster board should hold about twenty grapes. After the grapes are glued down, trim away the remaining poster board from the edges of the grapes. Continue creating bunches of grapes until all of the photographs are gone, using as many sheets of poster board as you need.

Hang the Grapevine Collage for all to see. The bunches of grapes can be connected together by twine or green crepe paper streamers. Hang a note from the twine or write on the streamer: "I am the vine, you are the branches" (John 15:5).

If you have the storage space, consider saving the collage after you take it down to bring out at a church event five or ten years later.

THE MITTEN TREE

Mittens and gloves are a perennial necessity for many as they tend to get lost, get holes, or get grimy! Plan to collect gloves and mittens for the needy several weeks before the first expected cold weather. Begin by putting an announcement in the bulletin and on the same Sunday set up a tree in the church. This tree can be a bare branch, an evergreen, or an artificial Christmas tree. Explain to the congregation that on the next three Sundays the church will be collecting gloves and mittens for needy children and adults in the community.

Before and after worship, worshipers may drape their colorful donations over the tree's branches. Mittens and gloves are usually attached at the cuff by a plastic or cotton thread when purchased and can therefore be draped over the branches without clips or clothespins.

When the Mitten Tree is fully decorated, box up the gloves and mittens and take them to a local school, shelter, or service agency, with love from your church.

GARDEN BOUNTY TABLE

The benefits of this idea are threefold: gardeners have the pleasure of sharing the bounties of their garden, fellow church members have the chance to take home their choice of the harvest for a small donation of money, and the donations of money are allocated to a mission project of the church.

In the spring, explain the Garden Bounty Table to the congregation and set up a table with a sign and a donation box. Decide where the donated money will go. A note in the bulletin and newsletter will help worshipers remember to participate, but the best advertising will be the Garden Bounty Table itself when it is filled with produce. In spring, lettuce and spinach, flats of seedlings, and bouquets of spring flowers can grace the table. As spring becomes summer, flowers, bags of berries, vegetables, and melons will tantalize the congregation. The autumn will bring dried flowers, nuts, jellies, herb and evergreen wreaths, divided bulbs, decorative gourds, and pumpkins.

Thanksgiving week is a good time to conclude the project and thank the contributors. Be sure to announce how much money was collected since the spring and remind the congregation of how the funds are being used.

SHELTER SUNDAY

Shelters for the homeless and shelters for battered women and children are in almost constant need of toiletries such as toothpaste and shampoo as well as paper products. Consult a shelter near you to determine what is needed the most. Ask too, if someone who works or volunteers at the shelter might be able to speak about the shelter and its mission for just a few minutes during a worship service. If this is not possible, request some information about the work of the shelter that can be relayed to your congregation during the worship service.

Select a date for Shelter Sunday. For a month or so ahead of this date, list the items needed in the bulletin and your church's newsletter. Purchase several colorful laundry baskets, useful for the storage of anything from toys to real laundry, that can be used to hold the donations and then sent along to the shelter as well. You may want to place the laundry baskets at the back of the church a few weeks ahead of time to hold the donations of those who may be out of town on Shelter Sunday.

On Shelter Sunday, as worshipers arrive, their donations can be placed in the laundry baskets. At some point in the service, introduce the speaker from the shelter or have a member of the congregation say a few words about the shelter.

After the service the guest speaker may take the baskets, or they can be delivered to the shelter by a member of the congregation.

BEYOND OFFERING PLATES

On occasions when a special offering is taken or when the worship service has a particular theme, it is creative and appropriate to use something different in which to collect the offering.

The ushers can take up the collection as they usually do, except that instead of passing the traditional offering plate, they will pass these:

Baskets: themes of harvest, Thanksgiving, Pentecost
Nets: stories of Jesus and the fishermen disciples
Backpacks or knapsacks: collections for camps, camp scholarships, youth outings or retreats
Soup bowls or soup cans: hunger relief or Meals on Wheels
Graduates' caps: seminary or other education offerings
Drawstring bags or purses: to honor the widow's mite
Antique bowls or pitchers: All Saints' Day
Treasure chests: "Where your treasure is, there your heart will be also" (Matthew 6:21)
Houses: Habitat for Humanity, denominational retirement home, orphanage, shelter, emergency or disaster relief
Shoe boxes: clothing fund for the needy or disaster relief
Crowns: an oatmeal box cut down and decorated to resemble a crown for Christ the King Sunday

Praise God if your creativity helps increase the offerings!

BRINGING FORTH THE OFFERING

In almost all churches, the offering plate is passed among the pews. To emphasize the idea that the money collected is an offering to God, choose a Sunday to have the worshipers bring their offerings to the front of the church. The ushers can stand and hold the offering plates as they face the congregation. If your church is large in size, you may want to use additional ushers and offering plates or baskets.

To make the moment even more significant, select a verse from the Bible that can be said by individuals as they put their offerings into the plate or that can be said to each person by an usher. The Bible is filled with verses appropriate for the occasion. These are from the book of Psalms:

For individuals to say: "The Lord is the stronghold of my life" (Psalm 27:1*b*) or "Teach me your way, O Lord" (Psalm 27:11*a*).

For ushers to say: "Look to him, and be radiant" (Psalm 34:5*a*) or "Love the Lord, all you his saints" (Psalm 31:23*a*).

Before the offering begins, carefully explain how it will be conducted and give any verse that is to be said. The usual choral response and prayer can be done after all have returned from bringing forth their offering.

TIME AND TALENTS OFFERING

Each of you must give as you have made up your mind, not reluctantly or under compulsion, for God loves a cheerful giver" (2 Corinthians 9:7). Sometimes it's hard to be a cheerful giver if the economy is weak, a town loses a major employer, or if personal circumstances are difficult. There may be various times when members of your church may be less able to support the church financially, but are looking for a way to contribute.

From another perspective, some members of the congregation greatly enjoy making a "hands on" contribution to the church, and feel that money alone is not a true sharing of all of their God-given gifts.

In recognition of the variety of ways that church members can be cheerful givers, develop a Time and Talents Survey to be used as an insert in the worship bulletin. Such a survey is especially appropriate for Stewardship Sunday or prior to a church workday. The survey will ask about times of the day, week, and year that are convenient to volunteer; technical skills; people skills; other practical abilities; tools, equipment, and resources to share; hobbies and interests; hidden talents; and even a pet project that an individual might undertake. The survey can also include a checklist of church needs.

Ask that the surveys be completed and placed in the offering plate that Sunday or the next. Help the congregation to remember that "There are varieties of gifts, but the same Spirit; and there are varieties of services, but the same Lord" (1 Corinthians 12:4-5).

After the surveys have been collected, share them with your church leaders.

COUNT YOUR BLESSINGS COLLECTION

The Count Your Blessings Collection asks worshipers to take a few moments to count God's blessings in their lives. Several weeks before the collection, request in the bulletin or from the pulpit that everyone bring ten coins to the worship service. You may want to have dimes that you can exchange for dollar bills available at the entrance to the church for those who don't bring change, and a bowl of pennies for those who may need coins but have forgotten their wallets.

Place an envelope in each pew with "Count Your Blessings Collection" written on it in bold letters.

When the time comes for the collection, the pastor or lay leader can explain the collection and its purpose: to remind the congregation of the many ways that they have been blessed by God. As a type of blessing is read aloud, each person should silently think of a blessing in his or her life that fits that category and then place a coin in the envelope as it is passed across the pew. Types of blessings might include:

- a happy childhood memory
- a loved one
- a pet
- a good friend
- a special outing
- a favorite food
- a quiet moment
- someone who has helped you along the way
- a song or book you especially like
- a favorite season

When the whole list has been read, the envelope can be passed one more time for anyone who has a regular offering to add. The ushers can then collect the envelopes, and, if not already the tradition in your church, the offering can be presented as the congregation sings "Praise God from Whom All Blessings Flow." The prayer following the collection might include thanks to God for the many blessings in our lives.

4. MUSIC AND HYMNS

FAVORITE HYMN CONTEST

Almost everyone has a favorite hymn. Why not take a vote and find out which hymns are most beloved among your congregation? First, select a date for a Favorite Hymn Contest. Then decide when your church will sing the winning hymns. You might want to use them in a hymn sing, sing one a week, or one a month.

Next, publicize the contest. Write an announcement for the bulletin or newsletter. Make eye-catching posters to place about the church. Make certain, too, that a word is said from the pulpit about this event.

This arranged, design a simple ballot stating: "Favorite Hymn Contest! Please write the name of your favorite hymn in the space below." Print the ballots in a bulletin or newsletter ahead of time if the congregation is to have the chance to mull over their choices, and ask them to bring the ballots back to church. Otherwise, bulletin inserts or small slips of paper are suitable for voting on Sunday.

Of course you will want to create a fetching ballot box. Consider old sheet music, musical theme wrapping paper, or craft paper with musical note cutouts to cover a cardboard box. Cut a slit in the top of the box for voters to cast their ballots.

On the day that the ballots are cast, be sure to tell everyone that the contest results will be announced in church the following Sunday. Also announce when the winning hymns are scheduled to be sung.

Once you tally the votes, a list of the fifteen or twenty hymns that receive the most votes should go to the pastor and the organist. The names of the winning hymns can be announced from the pulpit or in the bulletin. And, of course, everyone will look forward to singing the winner!

Save the ballot box and hold the contest again sometime.

BELOVED CHILDHOOD SONGS

Children often learn songs in Sunday school or children's church only to find that the songs aren't sung in the "big church." And adults, unless they work with children, never get to sing the beloved songs of their childhood such as "Jesus Loves Me" or "Zacchaeus." You can solve this injustice by arranging for your congregation to sing these songs in the worship service.

Consider using a children's song as a call to worship, as part of the children's sermon, after the regular sermon, during the offering, or following the benediction. Your choir director might enjoy working some of these songs into a medley. No matter when during the service the songs are sung, the children will like to be called to the front to help lead the singing and to teach the congregation any corresponding hand motions that they have learned.

Wee Sing Bible Songs by Pamela C. Beall and Susan H. Nipp (Los Angeles, Calif.: Price Stern Sloan, 1986) is a wonderful collection of Christian songs for children. The music is simply arranged and includes chords for the guitar and piano. The book also gives hand motions and scripture references for many of the songs. A cassette tape of the songs is also available.

A HYMN SING

Music brings expression and inspiration to faith and for centuries singing has been an important aspect of worship. To the very early Christians, Paul advises: "With gratitude in your hearts sing psalms, hymns, and spiritual songs to God" (Colossians 3:16*b*). Celebrate Paul's words with a hymn sing. Within your traditional order of worship, some adaptations can be made to turn the usual service into a hymn sing. Here are some suggested adjustments:

Preludes and postludes are most often instrumental pieces. On this Sunday, ask the choir to sing a medley of hymns. A children's choir could sing favorite childhood hymns, or the adult choir could select some best-loved hymns.

The call to worship can be choral, using a short hymn appropriate for the beginning of worship.

Sing the psalm, as many churches do, or select one of the many hymns from your hymnal that is based on a psalm.

Make the focus of the sermon the importance of music in Christian worship, or recount some of the tremendous stories of faith behind the writing of many hymns.

Sing a hymn as a choral response following the reading of the lessons or the sermon.

During the prayers, ask a soloist to sing the Lord's Prayer.

Sing a hymn as the offering is collected.

Finally, following the closing hymn, sing a hymn, or perhaps just one verse of a hymn, suitable for the benediction.

FIRST VERSE, SECOND VERSE

When children are present at a worship service, they enjoy the challenge of singing a hymn in an unusual fashion. On occasion, keep both the children and the adults on their toes by varying who will sing the first and second verse or how it is to be sung. Try these variations:

- The women, then the men
- One side of the church, then the other
- Over forty, under forty
- The choir and the pastor, then the congregation
- The adults, then the children
- With the organ, then without the organ
- Standing, then sitting

Worshipers may have trouble remembering instructions for verses past the first two, so sing the rest of the hymn in the usual fashion. At a more informal hymn sing, you may want to use variations on several of the hymns.

HONORING COMPOSERS OF SACRED MUSIC

Worshipers hear sacred music played on the organ and other instruments and listen to anthems sung by the choir, but often know little about the individual who composed the music. Biographical information about the composers of sacred music can enhance the listener's appreciation of the music itself as well as pay tribute to the genius of those who glorify God with musical compositions.

Your organist or choir director may be willing to select the music of just one composer to be used during a worship service. A brief biography of that composer can be presented at some point in the service or printed in the bulletin.

Encyclopedias and biographical dictionaries such as *The New Grove Dictionary of Music and Musicians* (New York: Macmillan, 1980) are ready sources of information, as are the liner notes to musical recordings. Publishers of music may be willing to send you biographical backgrounds of contemporary composers of music whose work they publish. Here are four composers you might choose to honor:

William Boyce (1711–1779) was perhaps the most noted British composer of his day. First trained as a chorister, Boyce studied the organ and embarked on a career as an organist. He was appointed Master of the King's Music and Organist to the Chapel Royal, a group of musicians who performed exclusively for the queen. His works include over twelve sonatas, eight symphonies, twelve overtures, and ten organ voluntaries.

George Frederick Handel (1685–1759), who by age twelve was the assistant organist at Halle Cathedral, was also a virtuoso on the harpsichord, violin, and oboe. Along with operas, orchestral suites, and music for the organ, harpsichord, and chamber groups, Handel wrote oratorios, the best known being *Messiah*. Handel's choral writing style made all the words clearly understood to listeners, setting a model for British composers of sacred music.

Johann Sebastian Bach (1685–1750) was the great genius of baroque music and the father of twenty children. Bach wrote over sixty volumes of music, most unpublished in his lifetime. Known for extravagant flourishes and strange harmonies in his organ and choral music, Bach's compositions reflect not only his musical genius but also his deep Christian faith.

John Rutter (1945–) is a contemporary composer of sacred music. Born in London, he began his musical training as a boy chorister and then went on to Clare College, Cambridge. As an undergraduate there, he published his first musical composition and conducted his first recording. Along with writing choral and orchestral music, he has served as the choir director at Clare College and founded the Cambridge Singers, a mixed-voice choir.

THE MOVABLE CHOIR

As you open your hymnal and begin to sing you hear it: a beautiful voice somewhere close by, singing along with you. The quality and strength of that voice make it easier for you to follow the melody. Wouldn't it be a joy to have the choir closer to the congregation from time to time? Try these ideas for moving the choir among the congregation during the worship service:

The choir members process in, but instead of moving on to their destination, they stop in the aisles as they finish singing the choral call. They remain during the call to worship or opening prayer and stay to sing the first hymn with the congregation around them. On the last verse the choir moves to be seated in the chancel or choir loft.

During the anthem, the choir or soloist moves to the area in front of the altar or communion table to sing.

The choir members can offer their special seats in the chancel or choir loft to a Sunday school class. On this Sunday the choir could sit as a group in the pews.

One Sunday, ask the choir members not to wear their robes and to sit with family or friends in the pews. As the service begins, it will be obvious that the choir is "not there." After the first hymn is sung, the pastor or lay leader can remark, "How lovely the congregation sounds this morning" and "Could that be because our choir is missing?" Then members of the choir can be asked to stand and receive words of appreciation for all their hard work and sacrifices, which include not being able to sit with their families. Then the choir can be asked by the choir director or organist to return to their proper place. Of course, the choir members will obligingly come forward!

JOYFUL NOISE

The familiar and beloved words from Psalm 100 call on all of the earth to make a joyful noise and to come into worship with singing and gladness. This means everyone, not just the choir!

Make a joyful noise to the LORD,
all the earth.
Worship the LORD with gladness;
come into his presence with singing.
Psalm 100:1-2

There is an easy way to draw the whole congregation into joyful noisemaking. Simple and inexpensive Joyful Noisemakers can be created by slipping about ten dried beans into a small envelope. After sealing the envelope, use a twelve-inch length of yarn or curling ribbon to tie a bow tightly around the width of the envelope. Tie the bow about two inches in from the end, so that the envelope is crimped into a fan shape. Sunday school classes or the youth group can be put in charge of preparing the Joyful Noisemakers. When finished, pile the noisemakers into baskets and on the Sunday they are to be used, have the children or ushers hand them to worshipers as they arrive.

Arrange for Psalm 100:1-2 to be read at the opening of worship, with the pastor or lay leader asking the congregation to shake their Joyful Noisemakers. Next, invite all to sing "All People That on Earth Do Dwell," which is based on and inspired by Psalm 100 and sung to the tune OLD 100TH. As the hymn is sung, encourage people to raise their voices and shake their noisemakers with gladness.

PRELUDES

As worshipers enter the church, they may be dealing with coats or umbrellas, looking around and greeting others, attempting to settle their children into the pews, trying to remember if they turned off the iron, scanning the bulletin, and finally, quieting their thoughts to become ready for worship. Music helps with this transitional time. Most worshipers appreciate the calming effects of the prelude and recognize that it sets a reverent tone. They are aware of the music, but are they directly focused on it as they would be for an anthem or hymn? Usually, they are not.

This circumstance creates an opportunity for choral and instrumental offerings by children and adults who are less seasoned or who do not have time to commit to a regular choir. By singing or playing a prelude, people are able to share their musical gifts with less stress and time commitment. With children and young adults consider an angel band, bell ringing, songs with hand motions or sign language, or liturgical dance. Adults may enjoy singing spirituals, rounds, shape note music, sacred chants, or contemporary religious pieces. Instrumental solos or groups will work well too, from the fourth graders just learning the flute to the adult who plays the dulcimer. To find willing musicians and workable ideas, place a note in your bulletin or newsletter.

HYMN HISTORIES

The stories behind many of the hymns churches sing are interesting and often provide quite touching insights into the faith of the hymn's writer. Before or even after a hymn is sung, the pastor or lay leader might want to give a bit of background information on the hymn, or this information can be printed in the bulletin. Below are brief histories of eight noted hymns:

"When I Survey the Wondrous Cross" was written in 1707 by Isaac Watts, considered by many to be the founder of English hymnody. When Watts complained to his father about the terrible hymns sung in churches, his father said, "Then write something better." He took his father's advice, and wrote over six hundred hymns.

"Blessed Assurance, Jesus Is Mine" is one of over two thousand hymns written by Fanny Crosby, who was blinded at six weeks, began writing hymns at forty-three, and died at the age of ninety-five.

"Rock of Ages" was written by Augustus M. Toplady after he took refuge between two large rocks during a violent thunderstorm.

"What a Friend We Have in Jesus" was written by Joseph Scriven for his mother and was never meant for public use. When a friend discovered it while attending Scriven at his deathbed, Scriven stated, "The Lord and I did it between us."

"Just as I Am, Without One Plea" is the work of Charlotte Elliott. An invalid, Elliott was left alone one day when her family went to a bazaar in town. While lying on the sofa, feeling desolate, she was overcome by a sense of God's peace, picked up her pen, and wrote this hymn.

"A Mighty Fortress Is Our God," based on Psalm 46, is in part, taken from Martin Luther's experience of being hidden from his enemies by Frederick the Wise at a real fortress, the Wartburg castle.

"Blest Be the Tie That Binds" came from the pen of John Fawcett, a Baptist minister in a small English town. Fawcett and his wife had the wagon packed to leave for a call to a prestigious London church. They were so moved by the weeping of their congregation and their own sadness that they unpacked the wagon and stayed. Fawcett wrote this hymn to commemorate the occasion.

"Amazing Grace" was written by John Newton, who had at one time made his living selling slaves. After becoming acquainted with a genuine Christian captain he changed from his sinful ways and became a minister of the gospel. He wrote this hymn in gratitude for the grace that saved him.

Check your church and local library for books of hymn histories. Kathleen Krull's *Songs of Praise* (San Diego, Calif.: Harcourt Brace Jovanovich, 1989) is a lovely picture book with music and brief histories of fifteen noted hymns. *Stories of the Christian Hymns* (Nashville: Abingdon Press, 1986) gives the background of over 125 hymns.

HYMNAL SURPRISES

When worshipers open their hymnals, surprise them with a small token or message tucked next to the hymn to be sung. Below are a few suggestions. As you leaf through your hymnal, you will be able to come up with other ideas.

"For the Beauty of the Earth" or "This Is My Father's World": a small pressed flower, leaf, or blade of grass.

"Away in a Manger": some hay or straw.

"Now Thank We All Our God" or "Joyful, We Adore Thee": a paper heart.

"Crown Him with Many Crowns" or "All Hail the Power of Jesus' Name": paper crown shape.

"Eternal Father, Strong to Save": a paper anchor.

"All Creatures of Our God and King" or "Christ the Lord Is Risen Today": slip of paper with "ALLELUIA" written on it.

"On Our Way Rejoicing" or "Rejoice, Ye Pure in Heart": slip of paper with "REJOICE" written on it.

Simple paper shapes can be cut from construction paper. Self-sticking notes will work well for words. Use a bold color ink and eye-catching lettering when writing words.

Sometime during the week of the service, place the surprises next to the appropriate hymn in the hymnal. This will take a bit of time but is not an awesome task if you have several helpers. A youth group may enjoy hiding the surprises and then watching, perhaps from the balcony, as worshipers discover them when the hymn is sung on Sunday morning.

5. GREETINGS, READINGS, AND RESPONSES

GREETINGS ON THE STEPS

Church members who volunteer to be greeters before worship are extending the right hand of fellowship to visitors, the faithful attenders, those who need assistance, the children galloping ahead of their parents, and those who arrive and sit alone. Whether your church uses greeters weekly, or would like to experiment with this idea, here are some good ways to recruit greeters, followed by creative ways to greet the arriving worshipers.

Recruiting Ideas:

Going down the membership roster guarantees that no one is overlooked; however, enlisting groups to greet is much easier on the organizer. Ask each church committee or commission to cover a month of Sundays. Also ask adult classes, and the men's, women's, and youth groups to take responsibility for a month.

Greeting Ideas:

Advent: Greet worshipers with the words of angels: "Greetings favored one! The Lord is with you" (Luke 1:28).
"For nothing will be impossible with God" (Luke 1:37).
"I am bringing you good news of great joy" (Luke 2:10).
"Glory to God in the highest" (Luke 2:14).
Christmas: Give a birthday candle to each arriver, saying "Jesus is the light of the world."
Epiphany: Welcome church members and visitors saying "Come and pay him homage" (Matthew 2:2).
Holy Name of Jesus (Sunday closest to January 1): Say with a smile: "He is named Wonderful Counselor, Mighty God, Everlasting Father, Prince of Peace" (Isaiah 9:6).
First Sunday in Lent: Greet all with Jesus' words: "There is joy in the presence of the angels of God over one sinner who repents" (Luke 15:10).

Palm Sunday: Give palm branches to each person, saying: "Hosanna! Blessed is the one who comes in the name of the Lord" (John 12:13).
Easter Sunday: Exclaim "He is risen!" to one and all (Luke 24:5).
Pentecost: To the arriving worshipers, speak Jesus' words: "Receive the Holy Spirit" (John 20:22).
Trinity Sunday (first Sunday after Pentecost): Hand a clover to everyone as a sign of the Holy Trinity. Say: "Welcome in the name of the Father and the Son and the Holy Spirit."
Thanksgiving: With a warm handshake, say: "The fruit of the Spirit is love" (Galatians 5:22).
Baptism Sundays and the Feast of John the Baptist (around June 24): Sprinkle a few drops of water on each person's hand, saying: "Be born of water and the Spirit" (John 3:5).

WELCOMING PENDANTS

Welcome worshipers at the church door with pendants for them to wear during the service. A symbol can be threaded through a length of yarn and the ends of the yarn knotted to make a pendant to go around the neck. Items to string on the yarn should be simple to make, or inexpensive, if purchased. As the pendants are presented to the worshipers, the greeters should quickly explain their significance. Here are a few suggestions:

Glad faces: Cut circles out of construction paper and add smiling faces. If children do the decorating, you are guaranteed delightful smiles. The pendants express the thought: "I was glad when they said to me, 'Let us go to the house of the LORD!'" (Psalm 122:1).
Bells: Purchase small jingle bells and string them onto yarn. Bells have been used to call the faithful to worship since ancient times.
Fans: Fold slips of white paper into small fans and clasp one end together with a length of yarn. For Pentecost, also known as Whitsuntide or White Sunday, the fans represent the sound "like the rush of a violent wind" that came from heaven to the disciples (Acts 2:2).
Candy canes: Tie small wrapped candy canes onto yarn. Candy canes are shaped like a shepherd's staff in honor of the Christmas shepherds.

SPEAKING HYMNS

Few will argue that hymns are a careful combination of music and words and are meant to be sung. Yet many hymns contain lyrics that can be used for a call to worship or a prayer. Worshipers will recognize the familiar lines of many hymns and may be touched anew by their message.

Usually, one verse of a hymn is a sufficient length for spoken use. Below are just a few of the hymns that work well. Enjoy looking through your hymnal and finding others:

The call to worship, or opening prayer:
"All Glory, Laud, and Honor" (first verse)
"All People That on Earth Do Dwell" (first verse)
"Come, Thou Almighty King" (first verse)
"Morning Has Broken" (first verse)
Before or after the confession of sins:
"Amazing Grace" (first verse)
"Blessed Assurance" (first verse)
"What a Friend We Have in Jesus" (second verse)
Closing prayer or benediction:
"God of Our Fathers" (last verse)
"O God, Our Help in Ages Past" (last verse)
"On Our Way Rejoicing" (first verse)
"Joyful, Joyful, We Adore Thee" (last verse)

The words of Lenten and Advent hymns are often appropriate for spoken use during these seasons of the church year.

SCRIPTURE SHAPES

Many choral readings and litanies can be written with a Bible verse as the response that is repeated by the congregation after each new line is read. To add a festive visual touch to these responses, make signs in shapes that relate to the Bible verse. Poster board or large sheets of paper can be cut into shapes. The Bible verse can be written on each shape in bold, dark letters.

Even the youngest Sunday school classes can stand in the front of the church and hold up the shapes during the choral reading or litany. Older children will be able to help make the shapes, perhaps embellishing them with marker or paint, as well as hold them up. Be certain to rehearse with the children so that they know to hold the shapes high whenever the response is said. You may want to use just one or two children, or an entire Sunday school class.

Here are some of the Bible verses that will work well as Scripture Shapes:

Stars: "Shine like stars in the world" (Philippians 2:15). "Praise him, all you shining stars" (Psalm 148:3).
Hearts: "I will give thanks to the LORD with my whole heart" (Psalm 111:1).
"You have put gladness in my heart" (Psalm 4:7).
Apples: "Guard me as the apple of the eye" (Psalm 17:8).
Feet: "Walk in all his ways" (Deuteronomy 10:12).
"Follow in his steps" (1 Peter 2:21).
Clouds: "Your faithfulness reaches to the clouds" (Psalm 108:4).
"Let the skies rain down righteousness" (Isaiah 45:8).
Butterflies: "I am the resurrection and the life" (John 11:25).
"See, everything has become new!" (2 Corinthians 5:17).

PSALMS

For God is the king of all the earth; sing praises with a psalm" (Psalm 47:7). Since Old Testament times, the psalms have been used in the worship of God. Today, most churches sing or read a psalm during the Sunday service.

If your church does not sing a psalm, ask your choir director to locate a simple chant that can be used to revise this ancient tradition. Chants are not too difficult to sing, but you will want to have the choir sing first to show the congregation how it is done.

There may be a soloist at your church who would sing a psalm. Many anthems and hymns take their lyrics from a psalm. Perhaps someone would accompany the singing with a lute, flute, or recorder as were used in ancient times.

David, the shepherd who wrote many of the psalms, could appear in simple costume to sing or read one of the psalms attributed to him.

Most simply, you can vary how the psalms are read such as having the pastor or lay leader read one verse and the congregation the next.

Centuries ago, Jubilate Sunday was celebrated when Psalm 66 was used as the introit. *Jubilate,* which means to "shout for joy" also refers to Psalm 100: "Make a joyful noise to the LORD." When these psalms are used, declare it Jubilate Sunday. Ask worshipers to begin the psalms in a whisper and let voices grow louder and louder until at the psalms' conclusion, they are shouting with joy!

READINGS IN DIFFERENT LANGUAGES

Throughout the Christian calendar there are Sundays that lend themselves theologically and historically to readings and prayers in different languages. The incorporation of different languages into the order of worship reminds worshipers of their heritage, the cultural breadth of the congregation, and their connection to Christians around the world.

The different languages are meant to enrich worship, not confuse it, therefore it is best to print the English translation of the call to worship, anthem, hymn, prayer, Scripture reading, or creed in the bulletin. Familiar pieces such as the Lord's Prayer or the Apostles' Creed won't need to be printed.

Call upon the congregation and members of your community who know another language. Here are several occasions when you might ask them to speak in a different language at your church:

Bible Sunday is celebrated the second Sunday in Advent. Have Romans 15:4 read in as many languages as is practical in recognition of the various languages in which the Bible is printed.

For the Week of Prayer for Christian Unity (January 18-25) or World Communion Sunday (the first Sunday in October) have the Lord's Prayer said in a different language or languages. Its familiar rhythm is recognizable even in another tongue.

On Good Shepherd Sunday (the fourth Sunday of Easter) have someone say the Twenty-third Psalm in Hebrew.

On Trinity Sunday (the first Sunday after Pentecost) or Christ the King Sunday (the last Sunday before Advent) use the Apostles' Creed in another language. As the creed is being said, ask the congregation to envision Christians saying it all over the world.

Also, special Sundays honoring overseas mission work or saints of the church may feature music, readings, and prayers in the appropriate language.

PASSING OF THE PEACE

The custom of the Passing of the Peace is a Sunday worship tradition for many congregations, while at other churches it is reserved for special occasions. The simplicity and sincerity of the Christian handshake cannot be improved upon; however, there may be times when the passing of a symbolic object from person to person may help strengthen the tie that binds.

Listed below are symbols of faith that can be passed among

worshipers, silently or with a few words. Depending on the size of your congregation, decide how many of the symbolic objects you will need. It will take about a minute to pass an object among thirty people. Before the Passing of the Peace begins, the pastor or lay leader should explain the significance of the object to be passed and give the scripture reference. If words, perhaps from the scripture reference, are to accompany the passing of the object, explain this too. The pastor, lay leader, or ushers should start by handing the objects to worshipers at various locations. Here are some suitable objects:

Keys: keys of the kingdom (Matthew 16:19)
Eggs: (hard boil first!): new life (2 Corinthians 5:17)
Butterflies (silk or paper): the Resurrection (Luke 20:36)
Bread (a small loaf): the bread of life (John 6:35)
Lilies: God's care (Matthew 6:28)
Chalices: Christ's self-sacrifice (Matthew 26:39)
Rocks: the church (Matthew 16:18)
Towel with basin: servanthood (John 13:5)
Nails: the Crucifixion (John 20:25)
Shells: baptism (Galatians 3:27)

When the objects have been passed throughout the entire congregation, the Passing of the Peace may be concluded with a simple prayer.

OFFERING THOUGHTS

Usually while the offering is being collected, an offertory is played by the organist. On occasion, give your organist a much deserved rest and present offering thoughts instead. Comb your church or local library for books of prayers, quotations, poetry, or devotions that contain thought-provoking Christian insights. Collected sermons, letters, and diaries such as those of John Wesley, biographical information on a noted theologian or saint, or accounts by missionaries may all contain suitable material. Even Christian calendars, children's books, and collections of light humor may provide just the right thought to read while the offering is being taken.

You will need about five minutes' worth of material. Thoughts can be excerpts from longer works or in other cases, you may need to string several short passages or quotations together.

HALLELUJAH RESPONSE

The words *hallelujah* from the Hebrew and *alleluia* from the Greek are recognized throughout the Christian world as words of praise. Hallelujah is translated "praise the Lord." In the Jewish tradition, the "Hallel" is a song of praise and thanksgiving to God. The traditional Hallel sung at Passover and other feasts is the combined Psalms 115 through 118.

Hallelujah appears again and again in the psalms, either at their opening or closing, rather like a call to worship. In the King James Version of the Bible, the word is translated "praise ye the Lord." In the psalms of the New Revised Standard Version, the New Century Version, and the New International Version, hallelujah has been translated "praise the Lord."

With all due respect to these translations, congregations may want to hark back to their ancient religious roots and recall the use of hallelujah from time to time. On those Sundays on which you choose to have the word *hallelujah* appear in the reading of the psalm, you may also want to use it in the call to worship or opening prayer, find hymns that use hallelujah or alleluia, and incorporate the word into other prayers. To further create a joyous feeling of praise and thanksgiving, banners and bookmarks with the word printed on it can be made.

The psalms using "praise the Lord" or "hallelujah" are Psalms 104:35; 105:45; 106:1, 48; 111:1; 112:1; 113:1; 115:18; 116:19; 117:1-2; 135:1, 21.

Even if you don't use hallelujah with these psalms, this brief history of the word may be a tidbit that will interest the congregation on another occasion.

SIGNING AMEN

God's word is spoken and written in many languages, including sign language. By drawing upon different languages and customs in worship, a greater connection and communion with Christians from various cultures can be felt. In the same way, Christians can demonstrate respect and understanding for the hearing impaired, who often feel isolated, by learning some sign language.

A simple way to bring about such interest and awareness among your congregation is to teach several signs that can be used in worship. Perhaps this worship experience will lead to a continued interest in communication with the hearing impaired.

Choose one sign at a time, introducing it during the gathering or call to worship or during the children's sermon. Then, ask the congregation to make the sign whenever that word is said during the service. Children are fascinated with sign language and learn it quickly. They will be willing participants.

AMEN (also PRAY): with elbows bent, hold hands slightly away from chest. Place the palms of the hands together and draw toward the chest with the head bent forward slightly.

PRAISE: clap hands together several times.

BLESS: make fists with both hands, resting each thumb outside against the closed forefinger. Hold fists close together in front of the mouth with the thumbs facing the mouth. Next, begin to open the fists as they are drawn away from the mouth. End with hands open, palms down, with arms extended in front of the chest.

CONFESS: place palms of hands against the body, with fingertips pointing down. Next, draw hands up and extend the hands in front of the body with palms of the hands up.

GOD: sign the letter "G" by making a fist with the right hand and extending the forefinger pointing straight ahead. Then, with the "G" hand, raise the hand up as if pointing to heaven. Draw the "G" hand back down to the chest and end by opening the hand with fingers together, pointing up, and the thumb lying on the open palm as it faces left.

JESUS: to show the nails in Jesus' palms, take the middle finger of the open right hand and touch the left palm. Next, take the middle finger of the open left hand and touch the right palm.

BIBLE: make the sign for Jesus, then make the sign for book by placing the palms of both hands together with the thumbs on top, then open the hands like a book.

6. ESPECIALLY FOR CHILDREN

BAPTISMAL OR DEDICATION KEEPSAKES

Babies who are being baptized or dedicated may cry or smile or even enjoy the attention, but chances are they won't remember this special welcome into the Christian church. Of course, their parents will one day tell them about their baptism. You can help by sending home a keepsake for each child baptized or dedicated at your church. Consider the following suggestions:

A photograph in a small frame: Ask someone to be the official baptismal photographer and take a picture after each baptism of parents, pastor, and child. The photograph can be put into an inexpensive frame and presented at a later date.

A book: Books make fine gifts for babies. Many Christian bookstores and catalogs even sell sturdy board books with a Christian theme.

A white rose or other white flower: The flower can be presented to the parents with the suggestion that it be pressed for the child's baby book or keepsake box.

A shell: The shell is a symbol of baptism. Present a seashell gathered from the beach by a member of your church or purchased from a beach or hobby shop. The date can be written on the edge of the shell with a fine point permanent marker. Also, many gift shops, especially at the beach, sell inexpensive items made from shells.

Christmas ornament: Purchase an ornament that can be unpacked, admired, and enjoyed again and again each Christmas season.

Any of these ideas can be adopted as a baptismal keepsake for an older child or an adult.

CRADLE ROLL SUNDAY

Cradle roll is a phrase borrowed from yesteryear, that refers to the youngest in the congregation. Oftentimes babies and toddlers spend the entire worship service in the nursery and are only seen by the nursery workers and a few others. Once a year, proclaim Cradle Roll Sunday and invite the nursery children into the service.

During the singing of the last hymn, ask parents to get their children from the nursery and bring them into church. The parents can hold their children as they, the pastor, or someone who works with this age group introduces them by name to the congregation.

Conclude with a closing prayer or benediction, perhaps incorporating one or both of these passages from the Bible:

"That you may tell the next generation that this is God, our God forever and ever" (Psalm 48:13b-14a).

"Let the little children come to me; do not stop them; for it is to such as these that the kingdom of God belongs" (Mark 10:14).

BULLETIN FUN

Many churches use bulletins for children that feature word games, dot to dots, and other activities. Kids love these bulletins and they are reasonably priced. Also, books of puzzles for children are often copyright free and can be reduced with the use of a copying machine to the size of a bulletin insert. You will need to keep handy a supply of pencils and crayons for the kids.

Another idea is to include challenges in the bulletin such as these:

Count: adults, children, lights, pews, windows
Design: new paraments or choir robes, a fancy cross, a bulletin cover, a banner
Copy: Christian symbols you see, a stained-glass window, a banner, the front of the bulletin or hymnal
Draw: the pastor, the flowers, the altar or communion table, the baptismal font
Listen and count: how many times you hear the word *Amen, Jesus,* or *Alleluia,* the number of prayers, the number of times you sing
Circle in the bulletin: the word *the* or *a,* all names, all numbers, all the B's or T's or H's

For any challenge that asks children to draw, have half sheets of paper available.

If the children enjoy the bulletin challenges, they may want to think of some themselves. When you print a child's challenge in the bulletin, be sure to print his or her name next to it.

A BIBLICAL THAUMATROPE

A paper circlet and two lengths of string create a "wonder-turner" that will amaze children and teach a Bible verse, too. A picture is split into two parts. One half of the picture is drawn on one side of a paper circle. Then the circle is flipped toward the viewer, and the other half of the picture appears. When the circle is spinning, the two pictures appear to the human eye to be one picture.

A thaumatrope can be made by cutting a three- to five-inch circle from sturdy paper or using a five-inch paper plate. With a pencil and ruler, lightly draw a cross on the circle to divide it into four equal quarters. These will serve as guidelines for punching holes and drawing or mounting a picture.

On one guideline, punch a small hole on the right edge of the circle, and again on the left edge of the circle, about ¼ inch from each edge.

Cut two lengths of string eighteen inches long. Loop one string in half and poke the looped end through one of the punched holes. Next, take the two cut ends of the string and thread them through the loop. Pull the cut ends until a knot is secured. Repeat with the other string and punched hole.

The next step is the creative challenge! Select an idea from the list that follows or one of your own ideas. The key to an interesting thaumatrope is positioning the drawing so that the two drawings (one on each side) make one picture. For example, "I am the vine, you are the branches" could be illustrated by drawing a bare grapevine on one side of the circle and writing "I am the vine" around the upper edge of the circle. On the flip side of the circle, draw branches of grapes that are positioned to correspond with the grapevine, then write "You are the branches" along the bottom edge of the circle. When the circle is spinning between the strings, the grapes will appear to be hanging on the vine. Some suggestions for drawings:

- Jonah and the whale
- Daniel and the lion
- A rainbow in the clouds
- The dove and the olive branch
- The door to the sheep pen
- The Star of Bethlehem over the stable

To make a number of thaumatropes, make photocopies of the drawings that can be cut out and glued in the proper positions on the circles.

SYMBOL BANNER BOARD

Explain the symbols of the Christian church during worship with a banner board, a new twist on a flannel board. A flannel board is usually made from flannel or felt, which serves as a surface on which to mount smaller cutout shapes. These cutouts adhere to the flannel board without glue or pins, making a quick, easy way to create displays.

To make a banner board, start with one yard of felt in a neutral color such as gray, tan, or black. You will also need eighteen inches of satin cord, eighteen inches of satin fringe, and a piece of cardboard seventeen by thirty-five inches.

Fold a thirty-six-inch square piece of felt fabric in half, so it measures eighteen by thirty-six. Glue or stitch the raw edges together along the length, then turn the fabric inside out. To finish the shorter bottom edge, glue or stitch the satin fringe so that it is secured between the top and bottom felt pieces. Next, slide the cardboard into the felt envelope you've made. Finish the banner board by inserting one inch of each end of the satin cord into the top corners of the felt envelope. Glue or stitch the top edge closed, giving the cord a little extra glue or stitches to hold it firmly.

Locate a place at the front of the church where the banner board can be hung, perhaps from the lectern. You may need to install a small hook as a hanger.

The symbols to be used with the banner board should be large, measuring about ten to fourteen inches across. Cut the symbol shapes from colorful felt or from white interfacing. Interfacing can be purchased at any fabric store, and makes tracing and detailed coloring with markers possible.

Here are some of the Christian symbols that may be presented and discussed with children at the gathering or call to worship, as a children's sermon, or as a tie-in to the regular sermon throughout the year:

trumpet	lion and lamb
bell	loaves and fishes
candle	bread and wine
angel	palms
star	the cross
three crowns or gifts	crown of thorns
a shepherd's crook	butterfly
sheep	alpha and omega
flames	ring

rainbow	ship
dove	anchor
triangle or trefoil	shell

The following resources, available at local Christian bookstores, will help get you started. *Symbols of the Church* (Abingdon Press, 1991), *Christian Symbols Pattern Kit* (Abingdon Press, 1989), *The Christian Christmas Tree* (Abingdon Press, 1988), and *The Christian Christmas Tree 2* (Abingdon Press, 1990).

SUNDAY SCHOOL MOVE ABOUT

Most children would enjoy the chance to move about during the worship service, experiencing the feel of the space from various locations. With the Sunday School Move About, each Sunday school class will take a turn doing just this. Some children under six may be reluctant to leave their parents' sides during the service, but older kids will respond with enthusiasm to this idea. The Sunday School Move About is also a way to honor each Sunday school class once a year and to make those students feel special.

Whoever conducts the worship service will want to plan the details and logistics of the Sunday School Move About, but it might go something like this:

The children begin the service seated with their parents. At some point in the first half of the service, perhaps before or after the psalm, the class is called forward. Ask the children to face the congregation and tell their names. Invite them to then be seated in the front pews, which have been reserved for them.

When the time comes to sing the next hymn, ask the children to sit or stand on the chancel steps to sing the hymn. If the organist is willing, the class could choose the hymn.

If the children are under ten, you may want to send them back to their parents during the sermon. If not, they can return to the front pews.

Toward the close of the service, ask the kids to come forward to stand with the pastor during the final hymn and benediction. The class may process out of the church with the pastor and then line up to shake hands and say "good morning" to worshipers after the service.

RAINBOW SUNDAY

Children love the story of Noah and his ark. The big ship, the great flood, the animals, and God's rainbow promise are all intriguing aspects of the account in Genesis. There are many possibilities for sharing the story of Noah and celebrating God's covenant as part of a worship service. Choose one, several, or all of these ideas to have a Rainbow Sunday for the children of your church:

Bulletin Covers: Children's Sunday school classes can color or paint rainbow bulletin covers a few weeks before the service. A simple line drawing of a rainbow can also be photocopied onto bulletin covers for the children to color during the service.

Toy Animal March: On Rainbow Sunday, invite children to bring a plush animal that they imagine might have been on Noah's ark. Have the children march, two by two, down the aisle with the animals. This march can be a processional or a recessional, or can be done at the time of the children's sermon.

Scripture Lessons: Genesis 6:5 through 9:17 is Noah's story. Other references to Noah include Matthew 24:36-39 and Hebrews 11:7.

The Psalm: Psalm 29 sings of the Lord's great power and glory, mentions the flood in verse 10, and asks the Lord's blessing of peace. Psalm 85 asks for God's steadfast love and salvation and speaks of God's righteousness and peace.

The Children's Sermon: One possibility for a children's talk is a discussion of the symbols of the story:

The ark, which saved Noah and his family from the destruction of the flood waters, has been likened to the church, which will save followers of Jesus on Judgment Day. Jesus makes this analogy in Matthew 24:36-44.

The dove and her olive branch were a sign to Noah that God's anger and punishment had ended. They represent the offering of God's peace, and the "extending of the olive branch" has come to mean "a peace offering."

The rainbow is the visible symbol of a new covenant between God and every living creature on earth. God promises in Genesis 9:16 that when he sees his bow in the clouds, he will remember the everlasting covenant he has made and will not destroy the whole earth again with a flood.

These symbols can be incorporated into a flannel board story, banners, bookmarks, paraments, or stoles for Rainbow Sunday.

The Benediction: Genesis 8:22 or Genesis 9:12-13 may be used as part of a benediction to close the service.

NO SEW LITURGICAL STOLES

A great way to teach the seasons and special days of the Christian year to children is with homemade liturgical stoles for them to wear. A stole for each child can be made with purple, white, green, and red cotton fabric such as broadcloth or kettle cloth. Use pinking shears to cut two-inch strips from selvage to selvage. This will yield eighteen stoles per yard. Pinking will give the stoles a finished look and prevent fraying. There is no need to line or hem.

When completed, sort the stoles by color and hang each color group over a hanger to prevent wrinkling.

On any Sunday that you decide to use the children's stoles, bring out the hanger with the correct color and place it in the back of the church. The ushers or greeters can hand them to children as they arrive. After the worship service, collect the stoles and rehang them.

These stoles should last for years, especially if they are reserved for school age kids. Consider bringing them out once a month. Below are the seasons and some of the special days of the church year along with the corresponding liturgical color:

Advent: purple
Christmas and Epiphany: white
Sundays after Epiphany: green
Transfiguration: white
Lent: purple
Easter: white
Pentecost: red
Trinity Sunday: white
Sundays after Pentecost to Advent: green
All Saints: white or red
Ordination and other church celebrations: red

The person responsible for changing the paraments may be willing to be in charge of the storage and handling of these stoles for children as well.

THE TRINITY STRETCH

Children often become squirmy during a worship service. Help them work out their wiggles with The Trinity Stretch. Here is how it goes:

In the name of the Father (arms crossed against chest),

In the name of the Son (arms straight out to the sides so the body forms a cross),

And in the name of the Holy Spirit (arms straight above head, then wiggle fingers as arms are moved slowly to the sides).

One Sunday, perhaps on Trinity Sunday (the first Sunday after Pentecost), teach children The Trinity Stretch along with a simple explanation of the Trinity. Then use it on occasion, as wiggliness demands. The Trinity Stretch, although fun, is not meant to be irreverent, and may even be used at the conclusion of a prayer with the participation of the whole congregation.

QUIET BAGS

When children ages two through six stay for the regular worship service, the little ones and their parents may appreciate Quiet Bags to help diminish the fidgets.

Quiet Bags need to be made of a soft material so they will not rustle when opened. Here is one way to fashion Quiet Bags:

Purchase pretty washcloths or dish towels (two for each bag) and thirty-inch shoestrings (one for each bag). Stitch two cloths together around three sides. On the open side, fold over a one-inch hem to the outside and stitch it down, leaving an opening at one seam to draw the shoestring through. Next, thread the shoestring through the hem to make a drawstring bag. These bags can be washed from time to time.

If you choose not to sew drawstring bags, large ziplock food storage bags will also work well.

A small assortment of non-noisy toys can be put into the Quiet Bags. Toys might include sponges cut into symbol shapes, squish balls, sock toys, felt finger puppets, and small cloth dolls or animals. The toys should vary from bag to bag. Above all, they should only make a soft "plop" when dropped!

Consider asking a craft or mother's group to take on this project.

7. PRAYERS

PRELUDE PRAYER CONCERNS

As the prelude is being played, many worshipers use this time for silent prayer. This is a good time to ask worshipers to focus on a prayer concern particular to your congregation: a church member who is hospitalized, a family facing a tragedy, a difficult decision the church must make, or a mission project. Prayer concerns might be of a less serious nature too, such as the youth group on a camping retreat or the new shrubs just planted on the church lawn.

Write prayer concerns on poster board or chart paper displayed on an easel in the back of the church or hung from the lectern. The concerns may also be printed in the bulletin. Ushers or greeters might mention the prayer concerns to worshipers as they enter the church, especially on the first Sunday this idea is used. Depending on the response of the congregation, you might want to have a Prelude Prayer Concern every Sunday, once a month, or just occasionally.

CLOTHESPIN PRAYER

Any one of us can count a blessing or think of something that we feel thankful about. For some of us, the thankfulness may be profound, such as the remission of an illness. For others, it may be as simple as being glad that the children didn't argue while dressing for church. Congregations can create an interesting and varied Prayer of Thanksgiving with a length of clothesline, colorful clothespins, slips of paper, and crayons. To do this, worshipers are given a slip of paper and a crayon upon entering church and asked to write a word or short phrase naming something for which they are thankful. These slips of paper will be clipped to the clothesline and read during the service as a prayer by the pastor or lay leader. The resulting prayer will bring a smile, a tear, a nod of acknowledgment, and a greater feeling of understanding among the thankful.

Plan a Sunday for the Clothespin Prayer. Decide when in the service the prayer will take place. Depending on the number of people attending the service, this may take a longer or shorter amount of time. Determine whether the clothesline can be easily strung in the front of your church or if you will need two helpers to hold it. To present the prayer, the pastor or lay leader will walk along the clothesline and read aloud each slip of paper. The congregation may say a choral response such as "Thanks be to God," perhaps after every third slip is read. If so, explain this in the bulletin.

When gathering supplies for the prayer, try to find a colorful clothesline and clothespins. Cut typing paper in half to make the slips of paper. Locate lots of crayons.

On Clothespin Prayer Sunday, place the paper, crayons, and clothespins on a table. Hang the clothesline. If the clothesline is to be held, show the helpers where they should stand while holding it.

Instruct ushers or special greeters to give worshipers a slip of paper, crayon, and clothespin when they enter the church. They should tell them to write, in large, legible letters, something for which they are thankful and then clip the paper to the clothesline.

If the clothesline is being held, it can be placed carefully on the floor and held up once again when the time comes for the prayer.

After the service, dismantle the clothesline. Clotheslines and clothespins are handy to have around a church. Use them to display the children's creations at your next Sunday school art show.

A VISUAL PRAYER

In sports, relaxation therapy, goal realization, and childbirth training, visualization is believed to be a successful mental technique used to achieve real results. Most prayer needs can be visualized as well. The pastor or lay leader should begin the prayer by speaking about the power of prayer. Next, the congregation is asked to think of a specific need or concern as the person leading the prayer pauses. Then, worshipers are asked to create a picture in their minds of the illness, sin, danger, sorrow, problem, or conflict that is troubling them. Each worshiper is then asked to repeat after the leader: "Lord, hear my prayer, see my problem."

The worshipers are next asked to picture the opposite condition or a solution: wellness, forgiveness, safety, peace, achievement, or resolution. The prayer leader allows a minute for the people to focus on this positive image, visualize it, and pray for it. The conclusion of the prayer by the leader will affirm and assure the worshipers of God's love and healing power.

WRITING PRAYERS

While not everyone is comfortable leading prayers during worship, there may be some in your congregation who would like to take a turn at writing a prayer to be used in a Sunday service. A prayer at the beginning of the service or the closing prayer or benediction are the simplest prayers to assign to others, but there may be some individuals who would write all of the prayers to be used in a service. Print a notice in the bulletin or newsletter and make an announcement from the pulpit asking those who are interested to speak with the pastor.

Groups can also write prayers to be used in Sunday worship. Children's prayers have a freshness and simplicity all their own. Consider asking each of the Sunday school classes to take a turn at writing prayers for worship. Youth groups, Bible study groups, and men's and women's organizations within your church may be willing to contribute prayers. Don't overlook a family, who could work together turning thoughts into prayers to be used in the worship of God.

LORD'S PRAYER POSTURES

Ask the mathematicians at your church to try to estimate how many times over the centuries the Lord's Prayer has been said. Then, to remember your Christian brothers and sisters of yesteryear, have the congregation say the prayer using a prayer posture of long ago. After a posture is demonstrated, ask the congregation to assume that position as the Lord's Prayer is said.

In the early days of the Christian church, prayers were said standing, as was the custom among the Jews. Arms were extended out, in line with the shoulders with the palms facing upward toward heaven.

In the Middle Ages, arms were often crossed against the chest. This posture was copied by a clever monk who baked the first pretzel to remind the village children to say their prayers.

Suggest to worshipers that they try two other centuries-old prayer postures at home: kneeling and lying prostrate.

JUMBLE PRAYER

The Jumble Prayer helps make the point that God hears the prayers of each and every person who prays. With the Jumble Prayer everyone fills in the blanks with a different response, and the words come out sounding jumbled. That's the idea!

The pastor or lay leader will read a line of the prayer and each worshiper will fill in his or her response. The prayer should be printed in the bulletin to make it easier to follow. Be sure that a clear explanation is given as to how the Jumble Prayer works and have the congregation practice filling in a line or two before the prayer actually begins. Responses should be given in firm voices.

You may want to write your own Jumble Prayer or use the one below, which is a prayer of intercession asking God's help for others:

Dear God,
>   Hear the voices of your people as we bring to you our prayers
>   for others:
>   We pray for someone who is ill: _____.
>   We pray for a friend who is troubled: _____.
>   We pray for a child who needs your guidance: _____.
>   We pray for someone who is facing tough times: _____.
>   We pray for someone who is far away: _____.
>   We pray that the words of our mouths and the meditations of
>   our hearts will be acceptable in your sight. In Jesus'
>   name. Amen.

PAPER PRAYER LINKS

Encourage the power of prayer and the depth of Christian caring in your congregation with Paper Prayer Links. As worshipers enter the church, direct them to a table where strips of paper (about six by one inches) and pens are in abundance. They are to write down a particular need or concern in their lives on a strip of paper. The prayer concerns may be signed or unsigned.

As soon as the prayer strips are written on and given to a helper at the table, that helper can begin taping or stapling the links together, creating a paper chain.

The paper prayer chain symbolically links all the worshipers together and can be brought to the altar or communion table during the worship service. Sometime before the close of the service, the pastor or lay leader can explain that the great paper prayer chain will be carried to the back of the church at the end of the service. As each worshiper departs, the pastor or lay leader will break off a link and give it to him or her. Those receiving a prayer link should pray for the written concern as many times as possible that day.

HAND-HOLDING BENEDICTION

Many families clasp hands when they say grace before a meal. One Sunday, have the entire family of your church join hands for the closing prayer or benediction.

You will need to think about the layout of your church to decide how this can best be accomplished. The choir may need to move closer to the congregation, those in the balcony may need to come downstairs, and those on the inside end of each aisle will need to join hands with the next row. It may take a few minutes to get everyone situated correctly. Ushers or an appointed "director" can help. When the entire congregation has joined hands, the prayer is to be said by the pastor or lay leader.

A PRAYER CAPSULE

Every congregation is a family of faith. As a family, the church's membership is committed not only to Christian beliefs but also to the care of one another and the care of the church. Like any family, a church family has old problems, new issues, differing opinions, many decisions to make, and much work to do. One Sunday, the pastor or lay leader can read from the letters of Paul that discuss the duties of believers and the church as a family of faith: Galatians 6:1-10, Ephesians 3:14-21, Philippians 4:4-9, Colossians 3:12-17, or 1 Timothy 5:1-2.

After the reading, the pastor or lay leader can explain that each member of the church family is to make a contribution to a prayer capsule. For the prayer capsule, everyone will write a one-sentence prayer. Along with the prayer, worshipers will write a brief pledge. Here is an example: "I pray that we will do more to help the elderly in our church family. I pledge to help weatherize the homes of these church members."

Worshipers will use slips of paper and pencils, located in the pews, to record their prayers and pledges. Parents may want to help their children. After a few minutes, the ushers can pass baskets to collect the slips of paper, then come to the front of the church and place them in a large envelope. The pastor or lay leader will seal the envelope, offer a prayer of dedication, and then explain that the Prayer Capsule will be "buried" in the church office. The Prayer Capsule is to be opened in one year.

In a year, open the Prayer Capsule and pin the prayers and pledges to a bulletin board. Invite members of your church family to read the prayers and pledges written a year ago.

A PRAYER REMINDER

January 18 through January 25 is the Week of Prayer for Christian Unity, observed in the last two decades as an ecumenical event. Originally Roman Catholics honored Peter on January 18 and Protestants remembered the conversion of Paul on January 25. The Week of Prayer for Christian Unity is framed by the celebration of these two great men of faith.

On the Sunday before January 18, explain to the congregation the significance of the week: This is a time to pray for Christian unity throughout the world, in their community, and in their church. Then, tell them to keep their eyes or their ears open for a midweek prayer reminder.

Use your congregational calling tree or postcards to send this message:

This simple call/card reminds
To pray for the tie that binds!

8. SHARING SERMONS

EMERGENCY VERSES

Oftentimes, just one verse from the Bible can be as insightful and thought-provoking as an entire chapter. Many Christians have a verse that they find to be especially significant to their personal faith. Emergency Verses is a sermon of sorts, a sermon made up of beloved Bible verses. This idea works well in an emergency situation, when the pastor is unable to preach. But on any occasion, a collection of carefully chosen verses makes a meaningful and interesting substitute for a traditional sermon.

In a situation when the pastor is suddenly unable to preach, perhaps due to a flat tire or the flu, fifteen or twenty members of the congregation can be asked to say or read a Bible verse. A lay leader can conduct the rest of the service. If the situation permits, these individuals can be phoned ahead of time. If not, they can be asked as they come in the door for the worship service. Most churches have a supply of Bibles on hand. In a church where Bibles are located in the pews, volunteers can be recruited from the pulpit. Ask those presenting verses to come forward, one at a time, to the pulpit. The Scripture reference for the verse should be given before or after the verse is read.

Of course Emergency Verses doesn't have to be used only in an emergency. If the pastor is out of town or your church is temporarily without a pastor, try this idea one Sunday. This is also a clever way to give your pastor a break from writing a sermon, perhaps as part of a birthday or anniversary celebration. Also perfect for a Lay Sunday worship service, this idea creates the opportunity for many lay participants to be involved in the service.

Youth group leaders may want to use Emergency Verses when their group is asked to conduct the Sunday service. The youth can be asked to bring a favorite verse to a planning meeting for the service. Asking each to say a few words about why they selected a particular verse can make for a stimulating discussion that encourages young people to talk more openly about their faith. This is also a good time to teach youth how to use a concordance to locate a verse of which they can only remember a few words.

However Emergency Verses is used, you may want to jot the Scripture references to the verses down as they are read in the worship service. Print them later in a bulletin insert or your newsletter. Consider, too, offering a small prize to any child who memorizes five or more of the verses.

YESTERDAY'S SAINTS

Congregations are continually evolving, and today's worshipers may not know about the exemplary people of faith who were part of the church in years gone by. These saints of yesterday will be remembered, of course, by some long-standing members. Ask these members for recommendations of Yesterday's Saints who can be honored during an upcoming worship service.

Oral histories should be recorded from church members who remember the people to be honored or who recall stories about them. Old church records, written histories, and albums or scrapbooks may provide interesting facts, anecdotes, and pictures. When all the information is collected, a tribute can be written to each saint's good works, dedicated service, and strength of faith.

If your church has quite a number of people to honor, the tributes can be given over several Sundays. When a date or dates are arranged, notify any family members of those being honored and invite them to the worship service.

The worship service that honors Yesterday's Saints can include passages from Paul's letters that refer to saints such as 1 Thessalonians 1:2-3 or Philemon 1:4-7. Consider singing hymns, too, that refer to the saints. A still life can be set up with any appropriate pictures or mementos. You may want to ask the invited family members to shake hands after the service.

Make this celebration of Yesterdays' Saints inspiring to all those who follow in the faith and footsteps of these past members of your congregation. Reflect not just on the honored with nostalgia, but give insights into their energy, strength, courage, and commitment.

A TIME FOR REST

The Hebrews celebrated the Sabbath on the seventh day of the week in honor of the day that God rested after creating the world. The Hebrew word *shabath* means to "cease" or "rest." Since Jesus rose from the dead on the first day of the week, the early Christians began to observe the Sabbath on this day. They remembered Jesus' words, "The sabbath was made for humankind, and not humankind for the sabbath" (Mark 2:27) and they continued the tradition of a day of rest.

What has happened to the Sabbath? Many churchgoers are exhausted by the time they sit down for Sunday worship: making breakfast, getting children dressed for church, teaching Sunday school or conducting church business before the service begins. One Sunday, instead of a traditional sermon, give a brief history of the Sabbath. Then invite the congregation to rest for five or ten minutes. The pastor should sit with the congregation at this time. Soft organ music will create an atmosphere conducive to quiet meditation. A prayer at the end of this period of rest might include the words of Psalm 46:10: "Be still, and know that I am God!"

TWO-MINUTE TESTIMONIES

Almost every Christian has a story of how God and faith have worked in his or her life. The story may be dramatic and distinctly memorable, or it may be a collection of experiences that span a lifetime. Set aside a time to invite church members to share two-minute testimonies as the sermon for the day.

With two or three months' lead time, announce that you are conducting a search for people in the congregation who are willing to speak for two minutes about how God and their faith have worked in their lives. Those giving testimonies may want to address one or several of the following:

- Earliest spiritual memory
- Experiences of faith that involve nature and the wonders of God's world
- A specific point in time when faith or a revelation seemed to strike like a lightning bolt
- A life passage that strengthened faith
- Testimonies of praise and thanksgiving to God

You should be able to find five to eight people to share their stories. Select a Sunday for them to speak. If your search finds a greater number of people willing to speak, set up several dates on the church calendar.

Consider using Paul's words to introduce or close the testimonies:

"So faith comes from what is heard, and what is heard comes through the word of Christ" (Romans 10:17).

"Now faith is the assurance of things hoped for, the conviction of things not seen" (Hebrews 11:1).

SERVING ONE ANOTHER

Most churches have a certain time in the year when new leaders take office and committees or commissions organize for the year ahead and recruit new members. Arrange a Sunday during this time when a representative from each church committee will speak for a few minutes. Contact these groups and explain that they will have the opportunity to describe their purpose, usual work, annual events, and any new undertakings. Each committee should choose someone who would be willing to speak at the worship service.

During the worship service, every representative will be called, in turn, to speak, after being introduced by the pastor or a lay leader. After the worship service, ask these representatives to stand with the pastor to shake hands with worshipers.

HONOR THY FATHER AND THY MOTHER

Although Mother's Day and Father's Day are not actually Christian holidays, many churches like to recognize these days set aside to honor two quite challenging jobs. This sermon idea asks for members of your congregation to speak about their mothers on Mother's Day and their fathers on Father's Day. You may want to ask ten individuals to talk for just a minute, or several people to speak for three or four minutes. Approach members of your congregation whom you think might be willing to speak, or place a notice in the bulletin or newsletter asking for volunteers. Those who agree to talk about a parent will appreciate this time to reflect on someone they hold quite dear.

Here are some specific questions the speakers might be asked to address:

- What is one special childhood memory that you have of your parent?
- How did your parent guide you in faith?
- What is/was your parent's most endearing trait?
- What one piece of advice from your parent will you never forget?

This sermon idea may become a Mother's Day and Father's Day tradition at your church. Over the years many people can have the opportunity to speak about their parents. Instead of a regular sermon, you might also opt to use this idea as a children's sermon, with just two people talking to the children about their mothers or their fathers.

SCRIPTURE CHARADES

Recruit some good sports to help with Scripture Charades. Participants should be given the verses they are to present ahead of time so that they can decide on the best way to act out the parts of the verse. During Scripture Charades the congregation will call out responses until someone says the verse correctly. The verse should then be repeated, loudly and clearly, by the person presenting the charade and the Scripture reference for the verse given.

Bible verses should be familiar ones. Not all verses are easy to act out as charades. Dig through books of Bible quotations or the Bible itself to find suitable verses. Here are some that are fairly easy to present:

"Follow me, and I will make you fish for people" (Matthew 4:19).
"Jesus wept" (John 11:35 KJV).
"Make a joyful noise to the LORD" (Psalm 100:1).
"I have fought the good fight, I have finished the race, I have kept the faith" (2 Timothy 4:7).
"I was hungry and you gave me food" (Matthew 25:35).
"Love the LORD your God with all your heart" (Deuteronomy 6:5).
"The Angel said to them, 'Do not be afraid'" (Luke 2:10).
"You are the salt of the earth" (Matthew 5:13).
"I am the light of the world" (John 8:12).
"He is not here, but has risen" (Luke 24:5).

Scripture Charades is a good sermon substitute for a less formal service such as a Youth Sunday, a lay person's service, or an outdoor or retreat setting.

A WORSHIP TOUR

Many people will attend a church year in and year out without knowing very much about the building in which they are worshiping. A Worship Tour will give the history behind the church building and then verbally guide worshipers through the worship space. History and anecdotes can be given about:

windows	baptismal font or baptistry
pews	banners and other needlework
paraments	plaques and memorials
altar or communion table	Bibles
lectern and pulpit	paintings and statues
organ and/or piano	candle holders

A still life display might be set up for this Sunday featuring photographs, documents, and other items of interest that help tell the story behind the church.

To prepare for the Worship Tour, research church record books, newspaper clippings, old bulletins, bills, and scrapbooks. Longtime members in the congregation may be able to relay information and anecdotes about the church unknown to the pastor and other members. These people may even be willing to give part of the tour. This idea is for new churches as well as older ones, and is as appropriate at a dedication service or a five-year anniversary as it is at a centennial celebration.

As the tour is given by the pastor, a lay leader, or several lay leaders, those speaking should stand by the part of the church they are describing. Conclude the Worship Tour with a prayer asking for God's continued blessing on your church.

QUIZ THE PASTOR

Questions play a role in the journey of faith for most Christians. Some of these questions are simple; others are far more complex. While your pastor will not claim to have all of the answers, he or she is trained in theology and will be able to help answer the questions of your congregation. Plan ahead to "Quiz the Pastor." Make a slit in the top of a shoe box, decorate the box, and label it "Quiz the Pastor." Place the box at the back of the church along with slips of paper and pencils.

Announce from the pulpit and print notices in the bulletin and newsletter that the pastor will be answering questions that are placed in the box. Leaders of Sunday school classes, especially the youth and adult classes, may want to encourage students to submit questions. Greeters and ushers can also help encourage questions and point out the box.

After several weeks, give the box to your pastor, who may want to answer all of the questions in one sermon, or address them over a period of time. At this point, the questions and how they are to be answered should be up to the discretion of the pastor.

Another twist on Quiz the Pastor is to have the congregation submit questions directly related to the pastor: What did you like best about seminary? What is your favorite book of the Bible? Why did you decide to become a minister? Many times the answers will give added insights into the life and faith of someone very dear to the congregation, your pastor.

EPISTLES

Many of the treasured words of the New Testament are contained in the epistles. For centuries since these letters were written, Christians have written letters bearing news, and giving support, guidance, and testimonies of faith to one another and to other churches. Continue this Christian letter-writing tradition in your church by asking various people to write open letters to the congregation on a particular topic. Ponder these possibilities:

Former Members: Contact those who have moved away. Ask them to describe their responsibilities when they were members of your church and to share what they appreciated the most about the church.

Past Confirmands: Write to those who were confirmed ten to twenty years ago and ask them to reflect on their childhood memories of the church.

Mission Workers: If your church supports organizations in the community, projects on a national level, or missions overseas, request a letter from each group asking them to update the congregation on the work they are doing.

A Testimony to the Pastor: Appeal to the pastor's parents, seminary professors, persons in the denominational offices, members of past churches, fellow clergy, and citizens of the community to write letters that remember and honor your pastor. Naturally, a lay leader should be enlisted to read the letters, which should be gathered in secret. Your pastor will be surprised and touched by these epistles. The letter testimonies are especially fitting for an anniversary or retirement and make fine keepsakes for a pastor.

9. HOLY COMMUNION AND FELLOWSHIP FOODS

SET ASIDE FROM COMMON USE

Most churches have a traditional communion set that they prefer to use when celebrating the Lord's Supper. There may be occasions, however, when something different can be set aside from common use for the holy use of communion. Consider these suggestions:

An anniversary of the church can be honored by using antique chalices and trays. Celebrate World Communion Sunday with international pitchers, goblets, and plates such as those made of Mexican tin, French glass, or Middle Eastern olive wood.

Communion cloths, customarily of white linen, can be occasionally exchanged for fabric of a different nature such as a festive batik, a country calico, or a Scottish plaid. For one communion Sunday, create a different atmosphere by using cloths of unbleached muslin that the children have decorated by dipping their hands into acrylic paint and making hand prints on the fabric.

Perhaps another Sunday, each communing worshiper could be asked to bring his or her own cup from home. This emphasizes the point that when Jesus first served his disciples at the Last Supper, they ate and drank from ordinary cups and bowls. During communion, worshipers should be asked to come forward, with their cups in hand. A small amount of grape juice can be poured into each cup. Be sure to have extra cups on hand for visitors and those who have forgotten to bring cups. The bread can be served from baskets or pottery bowls.

BLESSING CHILDREN AT THE LORD'S TABLE

Many children who are not yet old enough to take Holy Communion are left alone, feeling forlorn in the pews. During communion, invite these children to come forward with their older siblings and parents to receive a simple blessing. The pastor or lay leader can place a hand on the child's head or take the child's hand. A blessing such as "Child of God, grow in the love of Jesus Christ and the fellowship of this church" can then be said. The first few times that children are invited to come forward for a communion blessing they may be a bit shy, but soon they will feel a part of the celebration of this sacrament.

If your church serves communion in the pews, you may want to ask the children to come forward to receive a blessing at the end of the communion.

BRINGING THE COMMUNION GIFTS

In some churches, a family is asked to bring the bread and wine to the front of the church for Holy Communion. Take this concept one step further and ask families to bring to church the bread used for communion. The bread can be home baked or purchased from a local bakery. Families may want to bring ethnic breads such as tortillas, Ukrainian Easter Bread, or Native American Fry Bread.

The family will need to know how many small pieces of bread are needed for communion at your church so they can provide enough bread. You may want to ask the family to assist in setting up for communion, too. This is an excellent way to enable children to play an important role in the celebration of the sacrament.

Ask that the family carry the bread to the altar or communion table at a designated time during the worship service. The grape juice may be brought forward too, if served in chalices. Individual communion cups in trays can be heavy and are best set in place before the service begins.

A note should be placed in the bulletin telling which family has provided the bread and what type of bread it is. In time, your church may want to collect the bread recipes and print them in a booklet for the congregation.

AGAPE

Ritual meals that combine faith and fellowship are rooted in the Judeo-Christian heritage. The Hebrew Feast of Passover was a ritual meal for Jesus and his disciples as they partook of their last supper together. This Last Supper then became a sacramental meal for Christians.

The Agape, or Love Feast, comes from the ancient tradition of breaking bread to remember Jesus, to celebrate God's good gifts, and to strengthen the faith and fellowship of believers. In the early centuries after Christ's resurrection, the Lord's Supper was part of a larger meal or banquet shared by the believers and the needy of the community. This was called the Agape. *Agape* is the Greek word for a particular kind of love. In the New Testament it came to mean God's love in sending Jesus, and the love of Christians for one another.

By the seventh century, the practice of eating a regular meal along with the sacramental meal was largely set aside. Only a few religious groups maintained this practice. The Moravians, who immigrated to America from Eastern Europe, continued the celebration of the Agape, by then also called the Love Feast. This Love Feast included hymn singing, the reading of the Word, and testimonials of faith. John Wesley also practiced the Agape in the Moravian custom.

To continue this tradition at your church, set up tables in your fellowship hall. Schedule the Agape to begin toward the end of the worship service or after the service. Ask all to be seated around the tables and begin with the celebration of Holy Communion. After communion, the worshipers may be served more bread and grape juice along with foods such as fruit and cheese. The Agape may also include hymn singing and the sharing of stories of faith.

LAMMAS DAY

B read, the staff of life, has for centuries held symbolic meaning for many peoples throughout the world. One ancient celebration of the grain harvest is Lammas, or Loaf Mass. On this day, loaves of bread were brought to church in thanksgiving to God for the fruits of the harvest. You can incorporate Lammas Day into your worship service sometime in the late summer to praise God and to celebrate the earth's bounty. Here are some ways to celebrate this day:

Instead of flowers, place a loaf of braided bread, decorated with a lighted candle in its center, on the altar or communion table.

Give the worshipers stalks of wheat or other grain to carry as they enter or process into the church. These can be used as hymnal markers during the worship service.

Read Scripture that refers to bread such as Ecclesiastes 11:1-6; Matthew 4:3-4 or 6:9-13 or 26:26-29; John 6:31-37; Acts 2:39-42; and 1 Corinthians 10:15-17 or 11:23-29.

Ask worshipers to bring some kind of quick or yeast bread to present as an offering. Use large baskets to collect the bread. The various breads may be exchanged between worshipers after the service and taken home, eaten by the congregation at a picnic or coffee hour, or shared with a food bank or shelter.

BIBLE FOODS TASTING TABLE

O ne Sunday, set up a Bible Foods Tasting Table for worshipers to investigate after the service. A small table can be covered with a cloth. Burlap or muslin will look most authentic, and pottery plates, bowls, and jugs, and baskets lined with cloths will add a biblical flair. Several people in biblical costume might be on hand to explain the various foods. The Bible Foods Tasting Table might include:

raisins	mints
dates	grape juice
dried figs	pita and other breads
pomegranates	bitter herbs such as endive
olives	almonds
lamb	pistachios
fish	carob candy
beans	honey and candy made with honey

Have toothpicks, napkins, and small plates on the table. Small paper cups can be used to hold fish, beans, or other messy foods.

The authors' book *FOOD FOR THOUGHT: Thirty-five Programs for Church Gatherings* (Abingdon Press, 1991) contains information about many biblical foods. Recipes are included for such biblical fare as barley bread, bowl bread, lentil soup, and carob brownies. All of these foods can be served in small portions at a Bible Foods Tasting Table.

GATHERING FOR SAINTLY SNACKS

T hrough the ages, each saint has been remembered with a day of the calendar, and to each a particular plant has been dedicated. In some cases, a plant was chosen because it played a part in the saint's life story. Other times, it was selected for its shape or color, symbolic of the saint.

On the saints' days throughout the year, these plants were gathered for decorative and culinary purposes. For example, tansy was dedicated to St. Athanasius, credited with writing the Nicene Creed. The tansy's fernlike leaves and small flowers make attractive bouquets or wreaths. A tansy cake, popular at Easter time in days gone by, was thought to aid the indigestion that often followed a Lenten fast. Some plants have even been named for their saint, such as St. John's wort (John the Baptist) or herb Robert.

Today's Christians generally do not feel the same connection and devotion to the saints that their more distant ancestors felt. However, your congregation will find it educational and inspiring to spend a little time honoring the saints at a Gathering for Saintly Snacks after the worship service.

To do this, you can prepare brief biographies of some saints and print them on leaflets or posters. Books on saints may be available in your church or local library. One resource for your research could be *Butler's Lives of the Saints,* edited by Michael Walsh (New York: Harper & Row, 1985). To add a dramatic touch to the saintly gathering, consider dressing several people in costumes reminiscent of the saints being honored. These people could give short speeches on the history of the saints, create a tableau, or help serve the food.

The list below offers suggestions:

Salad Greens:
   Dandelion: St. Bridget
   Basil: St. Basil
   Cress: St. Barbara
   Turnip: St. Botolf
Fruit Salads:
   Strawberries: St. Hilary
   Cranberries: St. Faine
   Peaches and plums: St. Catherine
Salad Dressing:
   Add marigold petals, thyme, and marjoram to white
   wine vinegar. Mix in honey to taste. This combination
   is associated with a custom on St. Luke's Day.
Teas:
   Chamomile: St. Anne
   Rose hips: For all martyrs
Soup:
   Leeks: St. David
Bread:
   Rye: St. Benedict
Cakes:
   Anise: St. Erasmus
   Angelica (as decoration on Christmas cakes): St. Michael
   Honey: St. Gregory

These are but a few of the many plants and possibilities for foods linked to the saints. Books on herb gardening and herbs in cooking may serve as good references.

SUCCOTH

S uccoth, or the Feast of Booths, is a Jewish harvest festival celebrated for eight days in the fall. In Bible times temporary huts, tents, or other structures were set up to enable harvesters to take a respite from the heat. These shelters came to symbolize God's protection of the Israelites as they traveled in the desert.

In the fall, as a fellowship time after the worship service, celebrate Succoth by erecting tents on your church lawn. Perhaps your church or a member of your congregation owns a canopy tent. Tents can also be constructed using poles and sheets. Under this tent, set up a table for serving simple refreshments. Since grapes were harvested during Succoth, they should be served along with any other refreshments you choose. Here are some simple foods to consider serving: a variety of breadsticks, animal and goldfish crackers, raw vegetables, apple slices, cheese, pretzels, bagels and spreads, grape juice, lemonade, ginger ale, or cider.

Children, who adore tents, will be pleased if smaller tents, such as pop-up tents, have been set up just for them to enjoy while eating their refreshments.

Before the congregation is dismissed, explain the significance of Succoth and invite everyone to the harvest festival on the church lawn. A closing prayer might express concern for the homeless, who have no choice but to dwell in shelters that, for them, are only temporary.

TOAST AND TOPPINGS

T oast, a basic breakfast food, can be expanded into a buffet of toasted breads and tasty toppings. This simple idea for a breakfast before church or a coffee hour will appeal to both children and adults. Almost everyone likes toast!

Ask those planning the event to provide beverages and a selection of breads to be toasted: bagels, English muffins, scones, country biscuits, muffins, and all sorts of loaf breads. Request that worshipers bring a favorite topping for the toasted breads buffet. The request, printed in the bulletin or newsletter, can include suggestions such as honey-butter whip, Neufchâtel with fruit spread, grated cheese, peanut butter and other nut butters, jellies and jams, egg salad, pimento cheese, deviled ham, spinach spread, smoked fish, and pâté.

To cover the basics, those planning the event can provide butter, margarine, honey, and cream cheese.

To toast a lot of bread quickly, breads can be placed on baking sheets and toasted in the oven, several sheets at a time. Toast holds its heat nicely in cloth-lined serving baskets. You and your congregation will be amazed at the number of delicious ways that toast can be topped!

LUNCHING TOGETHER

Accounts of pioneer life in America describe families packing picnic baskets or lunch pails and then traveling to town for church. After the morning worship service, worshipers would enjoy eating lunch together. Oftentimes, they listened to several more hours of preaching before they left for home! Skip the afternoon sermons but revive the custom of spending lunchtime visiting with one another.

A simple way to serve lunch after church is with a sandwich tasting. Ask families to bring a sandwich for each family member and two or three extra. The sandwiches should be cut into quarters. The committee helping with the luncheon can arrange for drinks, plates, cups, and silverware. Chips, salads, and desserts are optional, but they do help to fill out the meal. In pleasant weather, you may want to serve on the church lawn, or serve from the fellowship hall but invite everyone to eat outdoors.

Worshipers can bring their plates of sandwiches to the fellowship hall before the service begins. The extra sandwich quarters should provide for those who are visiting, those who forget sandwiches, and those with good appetites.

On the Sunday of the sandwich tasting, at the end of the service, invite everyone to come and taste a variety of delicious sandwiches. Consider saying grace before the congregation is dismissed:

Dear God,
For bread and mayonnaise and mustard and butter, for ham and pimento cheese and roast beef and egg salad, for cucumbers and tuna fish and peanut butter and jelly, for all the sandwiches, and for this lunchtime together, we offer you our prayer of thanks. We pray in the name of Jesus, who broke bread with his disciples. Amen.

10. WORSHIP MEMENTOS

MYSTERY SCROLLS

As the congregation departs, send a Mystery Scroll home with each family. When the scrolls are distributed at the close of worship, explain dramatically that they are not to be opened until worshipers are back home. Mystery Scrolls are just right for:

Making an important announcement such as the start of the stewardship campaign or a new Bible study group.

Attention-grabbing invitations to an upcoming church event such as the annual picnic or vacation church school.

Sending home a special message such as a request for donations to the food bank or a thank-you for the congregation's support of the building program.

Using 8 ½-by-11-inch paper, write the message in elegant script, once on each half of the paper. Photocopy as many messages as you think you will need, cut the paper in half, roll, and tie with yarn. To give the scrolls a more ancient look, soak white paper in a pan of dark tea after the message has been photocopied. If you spread the sheets of wet paper on paper towels, they will dry in just a few hours.

POSTCARD GREETINGS

Paul writes in his letter to Titus, "Greet those who love us in the faith" (Titus 3:15). Help members of your congregation send postcard greetings to one another with this simple idea.

A month or two ahead of time, ask for donations of unused picture postcards. A box decorated with a few postcards can be placed at the back of the church or another convenient location to collect the donations. You will be amazed at the interesting assortment of postcards brought in by members of your church. If collecting picture postcards seems a bit impractical, purchase colorful four-by-six-inch index cards. Decorate one corner of each card with a sticker, a simple drawing, or a rubber stamp design.

One Sunday, hand postcards to worshipers as they enter the church. Have extra pens handy. Request that the worshipers address the postcards to themselves.

At some point in the service, collect the cards and explain what happens next. Each worshiper will be given a card when he or she leaves the church. Sometime in the next week or two, a word of greeting should be written on the card, then the card should be signed, stamped, and mailed. Children, who love to receive mail, should be encouraged to participate too.

Hand the postcards to worshipers as they leave the church, reminding them that Paul sent words of greeting to his fellow Christians two thousand years ago. If a worshiper receives the card he or she addressed, it should be traded in for another one.

A PENNY FOR YOUR THOUGHTS

This old expression is a familiar one to most people; therefore it can provide a fun springboard for conducting an informal opinion poll. The penny polling can take place at the coffee hour or anytime before or after the service when worshipers are standing about and visiting with one another.

The question asked should be interesting, but not of serious importance. This lighthearted survey can pose a question such as: When should we have our church picnic this year, in June or September? Or, when we repaint the kitchen, what color should it be?

Everyone should be approached: newcomers, old members, kindergarteners, and the clergy. Several volunteers can move among the people, carrying containers that hold lots of pennies. Curiosity will be aroused among the worshipers and they will enjoy being asked their opinions. Of course, after an opinion is given, that person will ceremoniously be presented with a penny!

After the penny polling, the volunteers should report to the person in charge the predominant opinions expressed.

ALL SAINTS' BOUQUET

On the first Sunday in November, honor all members of the church who have passed away in the last year. Do this with a beautiful bouquet of flowers, which will be divided among the families of those being remembered. Speak with the persons arranging the flowers and explain that within the large bouquet, smaller bouquets should be wired or tied together so they may be easily separated for presentation after the worship service.

During the worship service, as the pastor or lay leader remembers those who have died, he or she will tell the congregation that the flowers for the day are in their honor and ask that the family members of the departed come forward after the service to receive a part of the bouquet.

As the pastor or lay leader extends warm condolences to the families and gives them the flowers, he or she may suggest some options for using the flowers: placing on the grave, keeping in water at home for a week of prayer and remembrance, or pressing into a Bible or album.

INSIDE STORIES

Newcomers want to feel connected to their new church home. They usually study the newsletter and bulletin to get a sense of the church and what aspects of the life of the church interest them the most. There are many ways that congregations can reach out to newcomers to help them feel welcome, included, and informed. One idea to add to your church's efforts to make newcomers feel at home is a series of background stories about your church and its work.

These Inside Stories can explain current projects, the various organizations in the church, church activities and events, and how all of these came to be. Background information and anecdotes are especially important in helping newcomers feel a part of the traditions and customs of the church. Inside Stories can also include short interviews with church leaders and the pastor.

Inside Stories can be printed, one story at a time, and inserted into the bulletin or placed alongside newsletters and other handouts. One person may compile the stories or the assignment can be shared by a team. These stories should be as short and as easy to write as they are to read. As time goes on, Inside Stories can be slipped into a binder for the church library.

TAKE-HOME TREATS

Surprise worshipers who "have tasted the goodness of the word of God" (Hebrews 6:5) with one of these sweet treats before they depart:

Honey Candy: "Pleasant words are like a honeycomb" (Proverbs 16:24).
Chocolate Kisses: "Greet one another with a holy kiss" (2 Corinthians 13:12).
Rock Candy: "There is no Rock like our God" (1 Samuel 2:2).
Candy Hearts: "A new heart I will give you" (Ezekiel 36:26).
Saltwater Taffy: "Let your speech always be gracious, seasoned with salt" (Colossians 4:6).

BIBLE CARDS

A Bible card, like a prayer card, offers a message of faith printed on heavy paper. Like the prayer card, this handmade Bible card is meant to be tucked into a Bible. Make Bible cards, perhaps with the enthusiastic assistance of a Sunday school class or a youth group.

Begin with a Bible verse that suggests a graphic image you can use to decorate the card such as "Do not let your hearts be troubled" (John 14:1) for hearts or "I stretch out my hands to you" (Psalm 143:6) for hands. Next, you will need white or colored index cards. Cut the cards in half, across the width, using a paper cutter for best results. Below are two decorating ideas you can use, or try some of your own techniques:

Stencil: Fold an index card and cut a simple shape (heart, cross, fish, cup, bell) to create a stencil. Using a small amount of acrylic paint on a sponge or stippling brush, blot paint over the stencil onto the card to be decorated. (Applying too much paint will cause it to run underneath the stencil.) Lift off the stencil and repeat with other cards. Print the Scripture reference on the card in a creative fashion.

Crayon Resist: Color a simple design (rainbow, stars, sun) with crayon, being certain to rub the crayon very heavily. After coloring the design, and perhaps writing the Scripture reference, use watercolor to paint over the entire card surface. The crayon will resist the paint.

If your church has a name and address stamp, you may want to stamp the back of the cards.

At the close of worship one Sunday, announce that each worshiper will receive a handmade Bible card. The card is to be passed along to someone else, perhaps by slipping it into a letter or pressing it into the hand of a friend.

BACK-TO-SCHOOL PENCILS

H ere is a back-to-school idea that combines a worship memento with a short children's talk to be given the Sunday before school starts. Purchase new green pencils or tie green curling ribbon onto new pencils of another color. Make sure to buy enough pencils to have one for each child. When it is time for the children's sermon, or at the close of worship, call the children forward and begin:

Green is the liturgical color for this season. Green is also a color used in traffic lights. What does it mean when a traffic light turns green? (GO!) You are going to go somewhere this week. Where? (School.) Some of you are going to school for the first time, others are starting at a new school, and others are returning to the same school, but after a long summer vacation.

Did you know that God is going to school with you? In fact, God will be waiting for you when you get there, too. There is a verse in the Bible that says, "For the LORD will go before you" (Isaiah 52:12*b*).

If you are excited or scared or just a little bit nervous about the start of school, remember that God, who loves and cares for you, will be going too.

To remember this, since green means "go," here is a green pencil (or pencil with a green ribbon) to take with you when you go to school. (Give a pencil to one and all. Younger children may be starting preschool, and even if not, everyone likes a brand new pencil!)

STICKERS TO GO

Nowadays, colorful stickers are found everywhere. Doves, hearts, sheep, rainbows, crosses, and many other Christian symbols can be purchased in sticker form. With some planning, it won't be difficult to link a sticker to a season of the year, a hymn, a prayer, a Scripture lesson, a sermon, or a church event.

Stickers make fitting worship mementos. They can be given to worshipers as they leave the church and worn home on clothing or hands. Some children even keep sticker albums and will be pleased to add a new sticker to their collection.

ON THIS ROCK

Rocks: Their beauty, practical uses, and variations in type, color, and form have intrigued and inspired people throughout the ages. Rocks play an important part of many stories in the Bible and take on figurative significance as well. Paul proclaims in 1 Corinthians 10:4 "the rock was Christ" and in Ephesians 2:20 "Christ Jesus himself as the cornerstone." Jesus declares to Simon Peter at his conversion "You are Peter, and on this rock I will build my church" (Matthew 16:18).

To serve as a reminder of their daily connection to Christ and his church, one Sunday present every worshiper with a rock. These rocks can be collected by a fellowship group when hiking in the mountains or by those attending the church picnic. Perhaps your church has rocks in a nearby woods or a church member has a rocky backyard. Of course a landscape supply store will have a selection of decorative rocks or stones for sale. Rocks should be washed and placed in sturdy baskets.

Select a Sunday when rocks are referred to in the Scripture reading, sing a closing hymn that mentions rocks or stones, or present a children's sermon based on rocks. At the end of the service, as the rocks are distributed, a "rock verse" can be said.